OVERLAND

OVER

GREG MacGREGOR   *Introduction by Walter Truett Anderson*

University of New Mexico Press Albuquerque

LAND

THE CALIFORNIA EMIGRANT TRAIL OF 1841–1870

Copyright © 1996 by the
University of New Mexico Press.
All rights reserved.
First edition

Library of Congress Cataloging-in-Publication Data
MacGregor, Greg.
Overland: The California emigrant trail of 1841–1870 /
Greg MacGregor ; introduction by Walter Truett Anderson.
— 1st ed.
 p. cm.
1. Overland Trails. 2. California Trail. 3. West (U.S.)—
Description and travel. 4. Overland journeys to the
Pacific. 5. Overland Trails—Pictorial works. 6. California
Trail—Pictorial works.   I. Title.
F593.M254 1996
917.9404'4—dc20   95-32470
                         CIP

ISBN 0-8263-1703-0 (cl)
ISBN 0-8263-1704-9 (pbk.)

Duotone separations, printing, and binding
by Sung In Printing Company, Korea
Printed on 150gsm Velvet Art stock

CONTENTS

I would like to extend thanks to three people who have been most helpful in my completing this project. First to Tom Hunt for his suggestions early on of sites along the trail I hadn't thought of visiting. In fact, many I didn't know existed. Second to Don Buck for generously sharing his years of research relating to the location of sections of trail through central Nevada. And finally to my wife, Jo Whaley; from the beginning to the end she gave needed encouragement, insightful feedback on the photographs, and thoughtful analysis of my conceptual approach.

ACKNOWLEDGMENTS

Independence is a tidy city near the Missouri River, a place with amiable Victorian houses and an abundance of history. The history comes in two packages: Westward Movement history and Harry Truman history. Some of the postcards I have seen in the shops, touching both bases, proclaim Independence to be "Where the Trails Start and the Buck Stops."

GHOST OF THE ELEPHANT, GHOST OF THE OWL

*Walter Truett
Anderson*

I visited Independence once a long time ago for some Truman history. I took a quick trip over from Kansas City to browse through the Truman Library and stroll past the lovely old white house where Harry and Bess once lived. Then, more recently, I found myself going there again, this time in search of the trail.

As long as I can remember I have been vaguely aware of the great treks across the plains in the covered wagons. When I was a child in Nevada I heard old-timers talk of them and knew that was the way some people had arrived there. My mother told me stories about them sometimes, when I was hanging about watching her churn butter or bake bread in our wood-burning kitchen stove. She spoke of ancestors of mine who had come west that way, and about a child who had been born out there or had died out there, I don't remember which. I have warm memories of those times of listening dreamily to mother-talk, but I can't claim that I paid close attention to the content.

Years later, after our family had moved to San Francisco, I became aware of another, more exciting, history of the trail. This was the movie version—rifle-toting Indians up there on the ridge, the wagons drawn into a circle, the U.S. Cavalry arriving just in time with bugles and the flag as my colleagues and I cheered and fed ourselves fistfuls of butter-laden popcorn. That was far more interesting, but as I grew up I kind of forgot about it, too.

Yet something remained, a certain secret pride. Without really knowing much about the Westward Movement—about where the trails were, what the experience of coming west in the wagons had actually been like—I harbored a general feeling that it had been something heroic, and I was glad that I was descended from people who had gotten to California the hard way. It gave me a bit of what, in a more contemporary California, we have come to call self-esteem. And then recently I learned something that brought all my childhood ideas about the trail to life again, and somehow changed them.

I learned that the trail is still out there.

Its exact location has been pretty well mapped out—the main routes, as well as various cutoffs and variations—and, although much of the old trail has duly disappeared under freeways, factories, houses, and shopping centers, there are places between Missouri and the Pacific where you can find the tracks of the wagons. I first heard about this when I met Greg MacGregor, a photographer whose specialty, hobby, and primary obsession was the trail. For years, Greg had been out driving around in the back country of the plains and mountain states, photographing the trail—and places where the trail used to be. He showed me some of his pictures, and I was amazed to see where wheels had gouged so deeply into the ground, from wagon after wagon going in precisely the same track, that the ruts—almost a century and a half later—were still clearly visible.

When I looked at those photographs I experienced a feeling—a kind of longing, almost a hunger—that sometimes rises up in me when I find myself in intimate contact with the lived past. The mystery of otherness, somebody has called it; the wonder of contemplating what it might be like to be someone else, living in a different time and place. The particularly piquant thing about that kind of curiosity is that we know it will never be satisfied—the other will forever be other; we'll never really know how it felt to climb onto a wagon bound for California. Maybe it's that very sense of not being able to know that brings the tourists to Independence. Maybe it's what brought me there.

SWALES

Greg MacGregor had started out exploring the trail in the Great Basin states, near its western end, but I decided to go have a look at one of the places—jumping-off places, the pioneers called them—where it began. I drove to Independence and found the National Frontier Trails Center, a pleasant little museum and library located (so said the visitors' guide) "near a spring where pioneers camped, ate their biscuits and bacon and filled their water kegs before heading west." The center has easy-to-follow exhibits with maps of the trails. I listened to recorded voices that, when you pushed the proper button, patiently recited pieces of information about the Westward Movement. I looked at paintings of wagon trains, campsites, Indians, terrain. I admired remnants of old-time clothing, tools, cooking utensils. And I realized that the trail has another kind of existence. It is more than a fading memory for families such as mine, more than grist for the Hollywood adventure mills. It is also legitimate American History. People look at trail artifacts the same way they look at Plymouth Rock, the Declaration of Independence on display in the National Archives, the Civil War battlegrounds. That was a subject I would ponder later, in my own wanderings along the trail: What did it mean, what was it about this particular surge of human energy that merited such reverence, even from people who had no personal connection to it?

My plan was to start from Independence, that day, and follow whatever traces of the trail I could find, all the way to California. I would do this in three or four different segments, a few hundred miles at a time. I had been studying some of the maps and trail guidebooks, and I expected that with their help I could figure out where the trail from Independence began and what routes it followed from there. I also hoped to get some more information from OCTA, the Oregon-California Trails Association, the national club of trail buffs—people who collect the maps, visit the obscure little monuments out there on the plains, search for tracks and swales. (The word *swale* had never played a very important part in my vocabulary, but I soon became quite friendly with it.)

OCTA's headquarters are located handily just behind the trails center. I went out the side door of the museum, past the Pioneer Woman statue—there she stood in her sunbonnet, wooden bucket in one hand, facing bravely westward—into the little restored brick building and joined up. A most hospitable society, as it turned out: I was introduced to some of the members of the local chapter, who happened to have been having a meeting there at the time, and one of them—a retired airlines executive named John Leamon—offered to take me for a short drive along the trail's beginning and show me a few swales.

It was news to me that there would be any visible tracks so close to town. I assumed that all traces around here had long since disappeared under houses and pavement, and that I would not see any evidence of the trail until I got out to Nebraska, out where the caravans had gone for hundreds of miles along the Platte. But John knew better. The buck did not stop quite where we were, but the trails indeed started. We walked out to the parking lot and he pointed in a southerly direction. "Most of the wagons," he said, "went down there about a block and then turned left."

We got in his car, went down there about a block and then turned left.

"Right there, now," he said, pointing toward something. I didn't know what he was pointing at. "Right there they all kind of cut off that corner." I looked at the corner and, sure enough, could see it was rounded off. The streets were neat and straight—just as they had been when Independence was first laid out—but that mark carved into the earth, just shaving a touch off the corner, showed me clearly where wagons, probably hundreds of them, had taken a small shortcut as they started out from the town, a few feet subtracted from the miles that lay ahead.

My first track.

A short way up the hill was another remnant of the trail. We had to get out of the car, consult a map, sight up along a grass-covered slope, and there was a diagonal depression—something like what might remain if a good-sized ditch had been dug there once, long ago, and then abandoned to fill gradually with dirt.

My first swale.

We drove southward through the outskirts of Independence while my guide told me where the trail used to run, pointed out sights and landmarks. We passed through an area called Raytown. I learned that it was named after a blacksmith, William Ray, who had had a profitable business here—sort of a first pit stop for people needing wagon and harness repairs. John told me this was originally the Santa Fe Trail, which served from 1821 onward as the main trade route to the then-Mexican city in the Southwest, and that the later travelers to Oregon and California used to start out this way too—even though it wasn't taking them in precisely the direction they wanted to go—because it was a good way to get across the Blue River and out to the plain.

I asked John how he had happened to become a trail buff. "Maps," he said, looking straight ahead. "I just always liked maps."

As we drove along through the suburbs, past gas stations and fast-food places, detouring from the main street sometimes to make contact with where the old trail had been, I began to understand the logic of this particular route. Every road, even a modern ramrod superhighway, is more than merely the shortest distance between two points; it relates in some way to the terrain over which it passes, and it expresses a certain stage of history—how much people knew at a given time about how to get from one place to another. And here we were following the top of a ridge, winding along its crest as it gradually descended toward the Blue River, a tributary of the Missouri. The Blue was the first of many rivers the trail crossed or followed along the way. There aren't many places, I would find, where the trail went far without a river.

It began to sprinkle. I looked up at the heavy grey sky and it seemed enormous, stretching out forever toward the West. I couldn't see any of the country out that way

from where we were, but the cloudy sky served as a mirror image of it, warning me how great a space lay waiting to be crossed. The day had that ominous feel of the Midwest when it is cooking up thunder showers; the air was warm, the sky a rolling mass of huge dark shapes. It was early May. I was beginning my own expedition at about the same time that most of the wagon trains began theirs. They wanted to get away when the grass was high out on the plains—feed for the animals—and if they were lucky they would get across the Rockies and the Sierra before the first snowfall.

We turned back toward town to take a look at Independence Landing. The Landing, the river port, was separate from the town center. The town of Independence was laid out on a sort of bluff, high and dry above the Missouri and its occasional floods. The Missouri has wandered a bit since then, and when we got to the landing there was little to see except a thick green stand of trees where the riverbank used to be. The only structure visible along the bank was a cement factory. Not much of a historical landmark.

Later I got in my Toyota and started out on my own. That was the first of several trail-scouting trips I took, rambling through history, along streets and highways and remote dirt roads, sometimes with some old trail hand pointing out what was and telling me what had been. At one time and another I have been over the whole route. Up through Kansas, then following the long, dreary Platte across Nebraska. Into Wyoming and past Independence Rock—the place emigrants wanted to get to by the Fourth of July. Over the Great Divide into Idaho and then cutting off southward where the California Trail separates from the Oregon Trail. Down into northeastern Nevada—not far from our old ranch—then picking up the Humboldt until it disappeared at the beginning of the Forty-Mile Desert. Across the meadows of Reno and over

the Sierra near Donner Summit. Along the Yuba River and forest roads that lead past the gold mines and down into Sutter's Fort. I have followed those trails. I have, as the old-timers used to say, seen the elephant and heard the owl.

JUMPING OFF

Independence Landing, that quiet green place out behind the cement factory, must have been quite a scene a hundred and fifty years ago. Looking at it, I could imagine the banks lined with saloons, stores, and whorehouses, the dock busy with riverboats unloading their passengers and cargo. In a movie with a scene of me standing there meditating about the past, the sound track might have laid in ghostly echoes of cursing workmen's voices, heavy footsteps on a gangplank, jingling harnesses, perhaps the distant tinkle of a barroom piano.

I had been reading histories of the Westward Movement, and I had some idea by then of how towns grew up along the Missouri in the middle of the last century, perched on the edge of the open land that was then called Indian Territory, land that Manifest Destiny—in the person of several hundred thousand people, horses, wagons, mules, oxen, and cattle—was about to change forever. The Missouri was navigable for hundreds of miles west of St. Louis, and people bound for the frontier often chose to travel by riverboat to one of these newer towns, Independence or St. Joseph or Council Bluffs, and begin the trek that much closer to their destination.

Those riverboat trips saved time, but they had perils of their own: I had read about people who caught cholera and died on the way, or who lost all their traveling funds in a poker game. The boats occasionally sank. Some travelers—backtrackers, they were called—decided right there that they had seen as much of the elephant as they needed to, and turned home when they reached Independence. But most of them survived that journey with their health, money, and aspirations in reasonably good shape, and arrived ready to purchase supplies and be on their way. Some had their own animals and wagons shipped to the outfitting towns, but others purchased everything there—which of course helped turn the new towns into thriving places of business.

At first, Independence was known mainly as the jumping-off place for the Santa Fe Trail—the southwestward freight route along which traders hauled wagonloads of goods such as cotton and cutlery, and returned with silver bullion and furs and Mexican mules. But other trails were opening up in all directions, explorers and trappers wandering everywhere out toward the West. Traders were using wagons to haul huge loads of saleable goods out to the annual rendezvous on the Wind River where mountain men and Indians would gather to eat, drink, talk, and barter. Lewis and Clark had reached Oregon in 1805, starting out by working their way up the Missouri in keelboats, and several groups of trappers and missionaries traveled overland to the Oregon coast in the 1830s. But, prior to 1840, there was no direct trail to California. The only Americans who had ever reached it overland were mountain men such as Jedediah Smith and Joseph Walker.

Smith was a Puritan, and he was different from most of his colleagues in the mountain-man trade both for what he did do and for what he did not: He did read and write. He did not smoke, drink, or take a couple of Indian women along with him on his travels. Smith made it to California by a southerly route from Santa Fe in 1827, but he was killed by Indians a few years later. Joe Walker, a raw-boned Virginian whose personal habits were closer to mountain-man normality, found the Humboldt and followed it across what is now Nevada and got across the Sierra range— possibly somewhere in the vicinity of the Yosemite Valley—in 1833. That was really the beginning.

Soon Americans were talking about putting together expeditions to take their families to California in wagons. There were already American settlers there, mostly merchants who had reached California by sea, and the Mexican government was said to be reasonably hospitable to them. John Sutter, a Swiss hustler who claimed to be a war hero, had conned the authorities out of a piece of land near the Sacramento River and was eager to get more people settled on it. Newspapers carried speculative articles about the idea of moving to California, and there were clubs—such as the Western Emigration Society in Missouri—dedicated to putting prospective emigrants in touch with one another.

You really can't appreciate the full grandeur and tragedy and difficulty of the emigration overland to California if you don't also appreciate the monumental foolhardiness of it. At the early stages, the lack of accurate information was astonishing. There were no reliable maps, only a few scraps of information passed along from the mountain men, and lots of rumors. A few real trails were known: the route to Santa Fe, the trail the trappers used out to Fort Laramie and beyond, and then the passage to Oregon. But what else was out there? What kind of country, what potential routes cutting off southwest from the Oregon Trail? Curious rumors abounded, such as the story of a lake, out of which two rivers ran all the way to the Pacific. Even the accurate information that did exist didn't always reach people who might have been able to make use of it. John Charles Fremont, who explored various routes in the 1840s, claimed later that he had never heard of Jedediah Smith. Fremont's competence in these matters is a subject of some controversy—Ambrose Bierce once said Fremont had all the attributes of genius except ability—but, still, it's clear that nobody really knew if you could get a train of wagons to California, or what might be the best way to try.

So the first California-bound caravan assembled in Independence in the spring of 1841, full of hope and youth and ignorance: a group of restless risk-takers, not entirely clear about what they wanted but willing to go to heroic lengths in search of it. Pioneers, for sure.

John Bidwell, a schoolteacher from Missouri, was the real leader of that expedition. Another young man, John Bartleson, was elected its official captain about a hundred miles out of Independence. Bartleson wasn't all that well qualified for the title, but he wanted it badly and had several friends with him who said they would turn back if he didn't get it. Historians, taking no sides, generally call this the Bidwell-Bartleson party.

There were over sixty of them, by the time a few late-comers had caught up with the caravan on the trail. The party was overwhelmingly made up of men in their twenties, with a few wives and a few children.

In one of the best of the general histories, *The California Trail,* George R. Stewart quotes memoirs in which something is revealed about the motives of the people who went on this first wagon train to California. One of the young men said he wanted "to see something of Indian life, and indulge in hunting on the plains, and all that sort of thing." Another mentioned that he had read James Fenimore Cooper's novels and Washington Irving's books of western adventure. "What more could you wish," Stewart asks, "than fun, excitement, an extended camping trip, new scenes, and the bright face of danger?"

Some of the emigrants had small wagons, some had large ones. Some of the wagons were pulled by mules, some by horses, some by oxen. At that point nobody knew what worked best, and as it turned out nothing worked all that well.

They started out going south from Independence, on the old Santa Fe Trail, along the route that John Leamon and I would drive a hundred and fifty years later, and then they turned northward. Some histories say there used to be a sign there at the fork of the roads—pointing one way to Santa Fe and the other to Oregon.

The Bidwell-Bartleson expedition was, like so many of those that followed it, part disaster and part success.

The disaster started to unfold a long way from home, out in the Nevada sagebrush hills near where my ancestors settled a few decades later and started raising cattle. The caravan got lost out there looking for the Humboldt, endured much hardship, and finally had to abandon their wagons. The Humboldt isn't a hell of a lot when you have found it, and they may have had a hard time believing that this was the river that was supposed to keep them alive for the next few hundred miles. Leading their remaining horses, mules, and oxen—but gradually killing most of those for food along the way—they struggled across the desert and into the mountains toward Sonora Pass.

I have backpacked into the mountains along the route that desperate little group took. They followed the west fork of what is now called the Walker River, named for Joe the mountain man. There are no swales to see now, of course, because the party had no wagons left at that point, nor much of anything else. One of the women, Nancy Kelsey, eighteen and carrying a baby, crossed the mountains barefoot. But the survivors made it over before the snows came, feasted on deer in the foothills, and thirty-three of them eventually reached a ranch not far from the San Francisco Bay. To me the most amazing part of this history is that about a dozen of those went back east again the next year, and four of that group then turned around and organized another wagon train that reached California in the early winter of 1843—but again without wagons, which they had to abandon on the trail.

The first wagon train that was still a wagon train after it got across the mountains was a party of Missourians in 1844, led by a reclusive blacksmith named Elisha Stevens. Stevens was a remarkably capable man, and many historians believe the pass where he crossed the Sierra should be named for him instead of for the unfortunate Donners who came along a couple of years later. Although the Stevens party suffered incredible hardships, every one of the wagons and every member of the group survived the trip. In fact, with the addition of a couple of babies that had been born along the way, more of them finally arrived at Fort Sutter than had started out from Missouri.

The number of wagon trains to California increased over the next two years, slowed down a bit after news of the 1846 Donner tragedy reached the East, then picked up again and, of course, took off when the gold rush began. By the end of the decade that had begun with the nearly disastrous Bidwell-Bartleson expedition, wagons by the thousands were rolling westward every summer, bringing all kinds of people.

OH, PIONEERS

Although we don't have real statistics of who went west, it's clear that it was primarily a young man's game. A certain combination of physical stamina and mental immaturity was the best recipe for anyone (a) deciding to go west at all, and (b) surviving the trip. But there were children, old men, and women—not only wives but single women and widows. I don't know how many of those women were the sturdy, uncomplaining, sunbonnet-and-bucket types immortalized in the statue I observed in Independence. Married women—some of whom had not wanted to go west in the first place—had to perform their usual homemaking tasks such as preparing meals and caring for children under enormously difficult conditions. They seem to have found their own kinds of joys and challenges along the way: Dee Brown, in his book about frontier women, *The Gentle Tamers,* notes that women in their memoirs tended to pay more attention to the astonishing natural landmarks and scenery, and also that many of them used improvised cosmetics such as wax and cornstarch in an effort to conform to mid-nineteenth century standards of beauty. Apparently those valiant efforts were of little avail against long days of outdoor travel. One Californian wrote: "The poor women arrive looking as haggard as so many Endorian witches, burnt to the color of hazelnut, with their hair cut short, and its gloss entirely destroyed by the alkali, whole plains of which they are compelled to cross on the way."

It is hard to grasp the tremendous range of experiences that people had. Some were utterly miserable most of the way, the crossing blighted with sickness and murders and drownings and freezing and starvation, and others just seemed to have a fine old time. Sara Ide, who had been a little girl when she came west with her parents in 1845, wrote later: "To me the journey was a 'pleasure-trip'—so many beautiful wild flowers, such wild scenery, mountains, rocks, and streams—something new at every turn." Quite a few made the trip more than once. My great-grandparents Christopher and Martha Truett found their first crossing sufficiently pleasant that they later, as a young married couple, made a quick trip back to Iowa and then came west again. They lived for some years in California and then went back over the Sierra to take up ranching in Nevada and raise eleven children. Talk about restless.

Some of the toughest crossings were the ones made by Mormons, who carved out a unique place for themselves in the history of the West.

The religion got its start in New York, and Mormon settlements flourished for a time in the Midwest, but the followers of the Church of Latter-Day Saints had some violent clashes with their neighbors, and in 1847 Brigham Young took a party of explorers west in search of a new home. He got some help from Jim Bridger—another one of the famous mountain men—who had settled down in Wyoming with the Indian woman he called Dang-Yore-Hide and opened a little trading post. Bridger showed them to the Salt Lake Valley, about a hundred miles southwest of his fort, and Young decided that was the place.

No pioneer settlement ever grew with more speed and energy. The Mormons began plowing the soil two hours after they arrived, and in eight days' time had thirty-five acres planted in corn, oats, buckwheat, potatoes, and green vegetables. They put up log cabins and adobes and laid out a space for the temple. Later that same year, over 1,500 Mormon colonists came west in wagon trains, bringing more hands and more animals.

The Mormons were good organizers and hard workers, but their zeal to populate the new Zion led to some of the worst tragedies of the Westward Movement. In 1857 they found new converts in England and Scandinavia, hustled them straight to the jumping-off places and got them on the trail. There wasn't enough money to outfit these bewildered recruits with oxen and covered wagons, so the Mormon leaders had them make wooden handcarts to load with their supplies and wrestle over the trails. The handcarters had a song they were supposed to sing along the way:

For some must push and some must pull
As we go marching up the hill,
As merrily on the way we go
Until we reach the Valley-O

The first three handcart parties made the grueling walk with only a few dozen deaths. The fourth and fifth, which did not get on the road until early September, suffered horribly. They ran into hard weather as they got further west, and redoubled their efforts to try to reach Salt Lake. Some of the men pulling the handcarts simply died from exhaustion when they lay down at the end of a day. Some of the handcarters died from freezing and starvation and disease. Some died of hypothermia after wading through near-freezing rivers. Others suffered frostbite and had limbs amputated by amateur surgeons. There are no recorded cases of cannibalism among the handcarters, but some incidents came close. Sleeping in a tent near the Great Divide, a young woman awoke to find a boy trying to eat her fingers. Dragged out of the tent, he began to eat his own; he died before morning.

The Mormons suffered along the trail, but they also prospered along it. They operated ferries and trading posts, sent caravans eastward from Salt Lake to pick up junk discarded by other wagon trains. Many of the 49ers went west by way of Salt Lake, where they bought food and supplies. Some of the Mormons bought exhausted mules and oxen from the emigrants, fattened them up, and sold them to other emigrants a year later. Lots of California-bound tools, kitchenware, and clothing—and dollars—ended up in Salt Lake City.

So, while some of the pioneers aspired to get rich off of the gold of California, other entrepreneurs of various kinds did their best to get rich off the pioneers. Then as now, money-making schemes abounded. One particularly nutty idea was conceived by an inventor named Rufus Porter in 1849. He advertised that he would carry passengers to California in a steam-driven balloon that was to float them comfortably through the skies above the struggling wagon trains, while they rested and dined on gourmet food. He offered tickets at $50—meals and wine

included—and I believe sold a few. That project never got off the ground, but another frontier Edsel called the Pioneer Line actually started out from Independence. The Line's promoters offered to get their clients across the plains in luxurious mule-drawn carriages in under sixty days. It started out in mid-May of 1849 with 125 customers, and several things went wrong almost immediately. The first mishap was that the guide, mountain man Black Harris, died of cholera in Independence. As soon as the caravan was on the trail it became apparent to the passengers that the Line was not too well organized—not enough food, not enough mules to handle the men and their baggage. By the time it reached Fort Kearney in Nebraska it was close to mutiny, and at Independence Rock in Wyoming it went through a spectacular shakedown. The passengers had to discard enormous amounts of personal goods; diarists speak of clothes and belongings scattered all over the plains. Many of the passengers died along the way, and the rest straggled through in semi-starvation to California.

Conditions began to change markedly in the 1850s. There were more supply stations along the way, and people who came later had information gained in part from the disastrous mistakes of those who had gone before. The trail was improving—turning into several regular highways in California, where enterprising citizens of different communities built roads to encourage the caravans to come their way. Soon crossings in under three months were routine. There were periods of difficulties with Indians, such as the Sioux rebellion of 1854–5, and in any number of ways an overland crossing still qualified as an adventure; you could still say you had seen the elephant and heard the owl. But it was gradually becoming less hazardous. Soon stagecoach crossings were available—something like what the Pioneer Line had attempted—and in the late 1860s the railroad was rapidly reaching westward, until the link to the Pacific was completed in 1869. That was truly the end of the trail.

ON THE TRAIL IN THE 1990S

When I was in Independence I saw an article in the local newspaper about a man who proposed to get a group together to hitch up some wagons and ride the old trail to California, just like the pioneers. He got some publicity—which was undoubtedly what he had in mind—but he also got some blistering criticism from trail buffs who pointed out that a lot of the trail is under cement. Not only under cement, but also under houses and churches and shopping centers and factories and schools. It runs through parks and college campuses and, out in California, through the Sugar Bowl ski resort. There are a couple of golf courses that have visible swales covered with neatly mowed green grass. You can stroll along there quietly and take a look at them, but I doubt that a golfer trying to focus on a putt would appreciate a wagon train coming through.

So, if you want to follow all or a portion of the trail—something people do regularly—you have to do some improvising. At some points you can follow the trail by driving along the present paved highway, which is more or less right on top of it. At other points you can follow secondary roads that have evolved out of the old trail. And there are many places where the trail and the highway are miles apart, so that the trail seeker's game is to take occasional detours away from the highway, locate the old trail, hike it for a few miles or bump along it in your car if it's driveable—my Toyota has some deep scars on its underside from such adventures—and then return to the highway.

I took a couple of trail-scouting trips with Greg MacGregor and watched him make some of the photographs that are in this volume. On one of those expeditions we got as far east as Nebraska. Another time we took a shorter trip to Nevada to check out the Forty-mile Desert, the route across Truckee Meadows (some good tracks just outside of Reno) and a couple of the places where wagons were hauled over the crest of the Sierra. We also paid a number of calls on people who live along the trail.

In Nebraska, on a chilly October day with snow on the ground, we went out to the spectacular natural landmark called Chimney Rock and visited Gordon Howard, who runs an outfit called the Oregon Trail Wagon Train. He takes tourists on covered wagon treks complete with "pioneer cookouts," staged Indian attacks, Pony Express mail service for postcards to the folks back home, and prairie square dances. His property is a kind of pioneer theme park, decorated with wagons and stagecoaches, and his house cluttered with other souvenirs—beads, pieces of tools and kitchenware, bones. We sat at his kitchen table, drinking coffee while he brought out for our inspection a collection of items he has sifted from trail dirt. He picked out a knuckle bone, said, "This came from a pretty big hand—about your size," and laid it along the back of my finger. It was a perfect fit, enough to give me an extra shiver on what was already a cold day. He said farmers and construction workers frequently dig up bones along the trail. Sometimes, when new bones are found, historians go back to the old diaries and try to figure out whose body they had once belonged to.

We walked out to a field near Howard's house and he pointed out a circular swale—clearly visible under a light dusting of snow—that he thinks is the only existing sign of a place where people really circled up the wagons.

In Casper we looked up Lee Underbrink, an importer of Japanese motorcycles and a member of the OCTA board of directors, who took us out on a long tour across Wyoming, all the way to Independence Rock, telling stories along the way about the pioneers, and about taking chartered buses full of OCTA members out over these same dirt roads.

In Reno we looked up Harold Curran, who had written a book, *Fearful Crossing,* about the Nevada part of the trail. Harold turned out to be an old friend of some of my Nevada relatives, and invited us to his house to admire his own collection of trail souvenirs and Indian arrowheads.

An easy drive eastward from Reno is the Forty-mile Desert, one of the toughest parts of the crossing. It is the empty, sun-blasted space that begins where the wimpy Humboldt sinks into the ground, and ends where the caravans gratefully reached the next river—either the Truckee, or, if they went more to the southward, the Carson. It is one place where you can still find debris from the caravans. The emigrants all loaded up their wagons with barrels of water, which they discarded when empty. The ground out there is still littered with the twisted, rusted remnants of barrel hoops. Here and there you come across blackened spots where wagons burned. Sifting around in one of those, I found a handful of nails. I keep one rusted nail and a small shard of barrel-hoop metal on a bookshelf in my office—my own mini-collection of trail souvenirs.

As you walk across the bleakest stretches of the Forty-mile—cracked moonscape alkaline soil—you can see, every ten or twenty yards or so, a dark oval space with clumps of meager grass. It takes a while to figure out what those are: They are micro-ecosystems, marking places where animals dropped to the ground and died—weary, depleted oxen that, had they endured for a few more miles, would have caught the scent of river water and green grass. Not far from where we walked and considered that somber piece of history, trucks and cars rolled comfortably along on the smooth pavement of Interstate 80.

LOOKING FORWARD, LOOKING BACK

The last trail-scouting trip I took was the shortest one from my home near San Francisco: seventy-five miles up the freeway to have a look at Sutter's Fort. For some reason, in all my years in California, I had never been there—didn't even know quite where it was—and was surprised to discover that it's really in the city of Sacramento, about a mile or so from the Capitol building.

It's a big, solid, adobe-brick structure and yet, if you consider its history, a monument to the impermanence of damn near everything. John Sutter himself was a kind of postmodern character, a wanderer who invented for himself a new identity as a Swiss aristocrat. When he got his Mexican land grant, built the fort, and began farming in the surrounding area, he of course changed the local ecosystems and had an enormous disruptive impact on the Indian tribes. The fort grew into the beginnings of a city, a trading center, a magnet for travelers. John Bidwell, who had co-led the first caravan over the Sierra, went to work for Sutter and became his right-hand man. But the gold rush and the admission of California to statehood destroyed Sutter's little empire, and he ended his days in a suburb of Philadelphia, making periodic trips to Washington to try to get the government to compensate him for the land the American courts had taken away from him when they reviewed the Mexican grants. Bidwell fared better—went on to become a state senator, then a Congressman, and finally a Prohibitionist candidate for president of the United States. And Sutter's farm became Sacramento.

Traveling along the trail can be a disorienting, schizoid kind of experience: One moment you are pulled into the past, then a second later you are jerked rudely back into the present. Once in a while you even find yourself thinking about the future—or, to be more precise, about some combination of all three, as was the case one rainy day when I was following the trail in Missouri while listening to a radio conversation about whether the American pioneer spirit might be invoked to gain support for an expedition to Mars.

The day I went to Sutter's Fort, I came home and picked up an essay about the "new history" of the West, which seeks to compensate for the shallowness of the Hollywood version of the Westward Movement by reminding us of sexist inequalities, racist contempt for the people whose native land was being ravaged and taken away, cruelty to the long-suffering animals that pulled the wagons, destruction of the environment. The new historians are quite right, of course, and yet I hope the pendulum does not swing too far. Somehow it seems to me that, if we are to disturb these ghosts at all, pay any mind to the piece of the past that is engraved out there in the soil and interred beneath the city streets, we need to do it with a mature, steady eye that neither romanticizes nor condemns. Maybe doesn't even understand, but does make some effort to feel—to imagine compassionately, from a distance of time, an experience of a kind we will never have.

That's what I like about Greg's photographs of the trail: they stand right on it with both feet, honor its past and look clearly at its present—some parts of which are still incredibly beautiful, and some of which are incredibly ugly—and help us feel our way into the sad grandeur of the great rush of human energy that once flowed this way.

OVERLAND

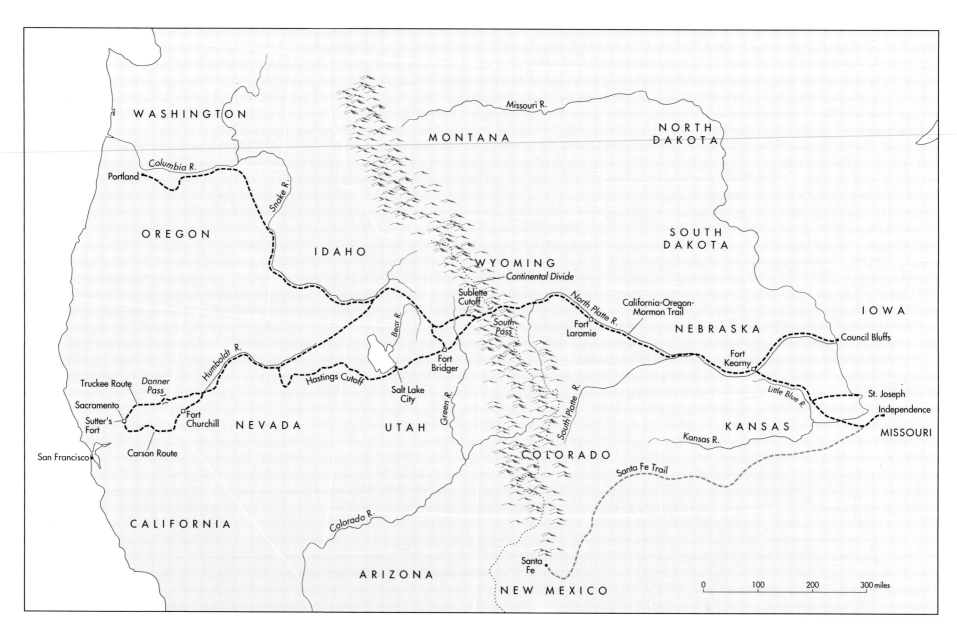

The Overland Trail, 1841–69

For the past fifteen years I have been traveling and photographing in the Great Basin area, that thousand-mile stretch of land—remote to most Californians—which lies between the Rocky Mountains and the Sierra Nevada. It takes its name from the fact that the region acts as a giant water sink. Its rivers never make it to the ocean and instead

PHOTOGRAPHING THE OVERLAND TRAIL 1

terminate in inland lakes, such as the Great Salt Lake, or just soak into the ground and disappear into huge marshes.

While driving the region's highways between widely separated destinations, I have often wondered where the road I was traveling would penetrate that far distant, yet approaching mountain range. I had a lot of time to ponder such matters, since the visibility can exceed one hundred miles. Almost always my guess was wrong, for just as the road seemed headed for a sheer wall, the river I was following made a surprise turn and coursed through a previously invisible passage, dragging the road with it.

My thoughts eventually turned to curiosity as to who discovered the first passageway into the Far West. How did they ever find even a remotely efficient route across a continent whose mountain ranges are generally perpendicular to the direction of travel? Once, while cresting a pass in eastern Nevada on an exceptionally clear day, I counted nine mountain ranges between me and California. Later, consulting a satellite relief map, I discovered there were actually twelve (I just couldn't see all 350 miles across Nevada.) Despite the uncooperative geography, early trappers and settlers did indeed find a relatively flat and nearly straight line route, some two thousand miles long. My curiosity was alive.

It took about one year to locate the original trail. No one I talked with knew about the historical groups, such as Trails West or the Oregon-California Trails Association, who for the past decade had been mapping, marking, and keeping alive the folklore and history of the emigrant trails. A library search turned up nothing. Undaunted, I began examining republished emigrant diaries, along with their crude maps, and attempted to locate the route based upon the written description. This simply did not work as it was too easy to miss a location by fifty feet because land features had been altered and the sagebrush was too high.

Two useful sources finally materialized. A guidebook to the trail, initially missed in my research, explained how to find the trail and follow it, mostly by using paved roads and the family automobile. Second, I discovered that on the detailed maps of the U.S. Geological Survey is often a small dirt track labeled "Emigrant Trail."

The problems unique to photography in desert areas were not unfamiliar to me, but some new ones did emerge. My methodology required me to follow the track and make photographs, no matter how visually boring the landscape might be. One must remember that early travelers were not interested in crossing the country by taking the most scenic route; in fact, the flatter the land, the better. The absence of vertical lines was particularly annoying, especially in those very remote areas where the trail is not disturbed by civilization, or even trees. Just to add visual interest and scale to the image, I soon began to focus on those places where the historic trail intersected with artifacts of contemporary society. Eventually, I photographed these intersections for the ideas they presented as well as for their graphic potential. After all, one can only make so many photographs of a pair of ruts going off to infinity through a flat sagebrush desert.

The romantic interpretation of landscape, often found in both paintings and photographs, has never interested me, and therefore I did not photograph it in that spirit. People used the land in the West to scratch out a living on a large or small scale by whatever scheme they could invent. In arid climates the evidence of these efforts is slow to heal, and it soon became obvious to me that the scars of the trail, together with the overlay of what has replaced it, would be a potent record of the meaning and current condition of the Overland Trail.

All the photographs were made standing directly in the ruts of the trail or looking straight at where they used to be. It was tempting to wander one hundred feet off to capture a spectacular image, but I resisted. The maps of the trail are very specific, and I followed them whether they led under concrete, through cities, or under water.

Even when the historic track was invisible, I often found a granite trail site marker erected by the local historical society or the Daughters of the American Revolution. Small towns remember their history, and marker placement was carefully planned. Someone, it seems, has always been interested in this trail and marked it with everything from hand-painted signs to bronze plaques.

I photographed the trail in sections, usually about ten days at a time. Some days I could travel two hundred miles, others only fifty, because I stopped to talk to a rancher about a section through his land. The conversation often led to a personal tour in order to clear up a point. Many times, the traces of the old trail gave out, and it was passable only on bicycle, which I used more than once, especially when a ranching fence without a gate crossed the track. Other times the trail just ended. In these cases, I backtracked out to the main highway and began another probe at some distance farther west. Since cattle were often in or near the viewfinder of the camera, my biggest job was to convince suspicious ranchers that I was not an advance-man for sophisticated cattle rustlers who needed photographs of their future booty.

The overland trail now passes through Forest Service and Bureau of Land Management land, factory and corporate yards, private ranches, and cities both small and large; much of the time it is under concrete highway. Restricted sites, however, were usually made accessible after I explained the nature of my project. The most difficult access I encountered was when the trail passed through Indian reservations, such as that of the Shoshone-Bannock tribe near Fort Hall, Idaho. Perhaps these Native Americans still remember the consequences of letting the first white man pass through their country.[1]

Ho—for California—at last we are on the way . . . we have really started, and with good luck may some day reach the "promised land." The trip has been so long talked of, and the preparations have gone on under so many disadvantages that to be ready at last, to start, is something of an event.

THE OVERLAND TRAIL: HISTORY AND OVERVIEW

At least two trips were made down into Missouri for young cattle for the teams. Then came the "breaking" process, which was accomplished by yoking them up and putting them "in the swing" between old Smut and Snarley (leaders) and Dave and Start (wheelers). It was hard to say which way ones sympathy should turn, to the young cattle, to the old, or to the drivers—surely commiseration was due somewhere. Then there were several trips to Lawrence (15 miles) for dry goods and food supplies. I got two pairs of shoes, calico for two spencerwaists, jeans for a dress skirt, needles, pins and thread and so forth. In the way of supplies there was flour, sugar, bacon and ham, tea, coffee, crackers, dried herring, a small quantity of corn starch, dried apples that we brought from Indiana, one bottle of pickles, cream of tartar and soda and that about made up the outfit. . . . All that trouble is over now, we are not worrying about what is ahead of us.[2]

Helen Carpenter, 1849

The California-Oregon Trail is a two-thousand-mile-long trace across the country by which an estimated 300,000 to 500,000 emigrants traveled to settle California and Oregon between 1841 and 1869. Most migration along it ended when the first transcontinental railroad, which generally paralleled the route, was completed in 1869. The trail began in several "jumping off places" (Independence or St. Joseph, Missouri, or Council Bluffs, Iowa), converged quickly, and then followed one river system after another until it terminated in either the Sacramento Valley, California, or the Willamette Valley, Oregon. The California and Oregon trails were identical (along with the Mormon Trail) for much of the way to a point just north of the Great Salt Lake, where the California travelers turned southwest to cross Nevada along the Humboldt River. The Oregon Trail continued westward along the Snake River.

The emigrants were diligent record-keepers. They kept accurate diaries of the miles driven daily, routes, campsites, illnesses and deaths, notable events, encounters with Indians and other travelers, and their reactions to what many considered an epic journey. Consequently, historians have had little trouble piecing together an accurate description of the migration. For these rich accounts readers are referred to such classics as George Stewart's *The California Trail* (1962), Merrill Mattes's *The Great Platte River*

Road (1969), John D. Unruh's *The Plains Across* (1979), and J. S. Holliday's *The World Rushed In* (1981). These works were compiled in part from the hundreds of published and unpublished diaries and tens of thousands of letters left by the overland migrants.

The crossing usually took five or six months by wagon, with the pioneers traveling between ten and fifteen miles per day. The overlanders timed their departure from the Middle West for early April or May, just after the spring thaw, when there was usually enough grass on the prairies for the draft animals to eat. They could tarry little however, for they had to cross the rugged Sierra Nevada before the first snow fell in late October or early November.

For the entire way, the overland trail followed major and minor river systems—a necessity for the draft animals. It began along the Big Blue River in Kansas and then switched to the gateway to the Rocky Mountain West, the Platte and North Platte rivers. This gently uphill path along the riverway headed in a nearly straight line across Nebraska and half of Wyoming. In Wyoming, travelers shifted to the Sweetwater, which they followed almost to the Continental Divide. This historic point, at the south end of the Wind River mountain range, called South Pass, is almost flat grassland, even though it is at an altitude of 7,000 feet. So wide and gentle is South Pass that most emigrants, and even today's travelers, cannot detect its summit across the crest of the Rocky Mountains.

Once across the pass, travelers encountered truly desert terrain for the first time. This high desert section of the trail headed southwest, crossing the Big Sandy and Green rivers and following the Blacks Fork River into Fort Bridger, Wyoming. At this point, the California and Oregon-bound settlers continued on the main trail northwestward, while the Mormon contingent headed due west down the nearest canyon into the Salt Lake Valley.

By diverting north, some 150 miles in the wrong direction California travelers could take advantage of yet another river system, up the Bear Valley and around the northern end of the Wasatch Mountains of Utah, an easy way off the high desert plateau that eventually connected with the Snake River near present-day Pocatello, Idaho. Migrants headed for Oregon could continue along the Snake all the way to the Pacific Northwest. California-bound emigrants considered this "detour" northwestward into Idaho to be a delay and nuisance, and at least two cut-offs were available to the foolish or impatient. In the end they rarely saved any time.

About thirty miles west of Pocatello, at an insignificant spot of land where the Raft River (now dry) meets the Snake, the California trail diverged southwestward to join the Humboldt River near Wells, Nevada. This barely flowing pool of brackish water, 20 feet wide, 6 inches deep, and 350 miles long, made crossing Nevada possible. The water was barely drinkable, there were no fish, and the banks contained choking dust. The one saving feature of the Humboldt was that it headed on a diagonal toward Sacramento, crossing almost the entire state of Nevada before disappearing into the ground at a marshy sink near present-day Lovelock.

Beyond the Humboldt, for the first time in seventeen hundred miles of travel, the pioneers had no river system to follow. They had a choice of two forty-mile desert crossings, one joining the Carson and the other the Truckee River, either of which could be ascended into the Sierra Nevada of California. The drama of this last parched crossing, when people, animals, and supplies were exhausted, was told and retold in every overlander's recollections. The loss of human life, livestock, and property was epic. Accounts tell of so many dead oxen that one could walk from body to body and never touch the ground. For years after, junk dealers from Reno scavenged this section to collect the abandoned iron for re-

sale. Some isolated sections of the trail still contain debris left by panicked migrants of a century and a half ago.

The overlanders' final obstacle was the precipitous east face of the Sierra Nevada. The first wagon to accomplish the ascent did so in 1844, in the Stevens Party, which had entered the Sierra up the Truckee River. The feat did, however, take two travel seasons, and the wagon had to be hauled over the top in pieces and then reassembled. This pass, now known as Donner Pass, was soon abandoned for an easier route, about one mile south along the same ridge and through present-day Sugar Bowl ski resort.

Although some pioneers, especially during the Gold Rush, returned to their eastern homes via the Overland Trail, the overwhelming bulk of travelers moved from east to west. Had they traveled in the opposite direction, the most difficult sections would have been encountered first, when enthusiasm and animals were fresh. Most emigrants made it to the "promised land," even though many perished or were forced to turn back. It is estimated that, averaged over the entire length of the trail, one person died for every hundred yards (most deaths resulted from cholera). Still, nearly half a million people survived the wearisome journey to begin their lives in the West.[3]

Emigration to California was sparse in the first few years prior to the gold rush. The list below shows the dramatic change.

1841	33 emigrants
1842	0 emigrants
1843	25 emigrants
1844–45	40 wagons (average four emigrants per wagon)
1846	200 emigrants
1847	90 wagons (average four emigrants per wagon)
1848	500 emigrants

1849   25,000 emigrants
1850   45,000 emigrants
1851   1,000+ emigrants
1852   52,000 emigrants
1853   30,000 emigrants + 160,000 animals[4]

The slump in the immigration of 1851 was caused by the horror stories from the previous year of lost wagons in the Nevada deserts. In addition, many unlucky and broke goldseekers had returned East and spread the word of their misfortune. Finally, a new land giveaway policy was instituted in Oregon which diverted most of the traffic into that territory. The significant rise in the number of animals crossing over in the early 1850s was caused by a shift in interest away from the gold fields to the rich farming and grazing lands of the Central Valley in California. Discovery of gold was, of course, the reason the flood gates to California opened in 1849, and men were not the only ones attracted to the idea of migrating to the goldfields. It is estimated that approximately 3,000 women and 1,500 children crossed overland in 1849.

Thursday April 18, 1850. We came at night to the house of Mr. McKinney . . . and were very hospitably welcomed. Mrs McKinney had a nephew who went to California in 1849, and she told me the wonderful tales of the abundance of gold that she had heard: that they kept flour scoops to scoop the gold out of the barrels that they kept it in, and that you could soon get all you needed for the rest of your life. And as for a woman, if she could cook at all, she could get $16.00 per week for each man that she cooked for, and the only cooking required to be done was just to boil meat and potatoes and serve them on a big chip of wood, instead of a plate, and the boarder furnished the provisions. I began at once to figure up in my mind how many men I could cook for, if there should be no better way of making money.[5]

Margaret Frink, 1850

Compared to the Oregon Trail, the California trail took longer to discover because there were no fur traders to pave the way. Its route was a complete mystery to the first group of emigrants in 1841. John Bidwell, a twenty-one-year-old leader of the first attempt to take a wagon train to California writes:

Our ignorance of the route was complete. We knew that California lay west, and that was the extent of our knowledge. Some of the maps consulted, supposed of course to be correct, showed a lake in the vicinity of where Salt Lake now is; it was represented as a long lake, three or four hundred miles in extent, narrow and with two outlets, both running into the Pacific Ocean, either apparently larger than the Mississippi River. An intelligent man with whom I boarded—Elam Brown, who till recently lived in California, dying when over ninety years of age—possessed a map that showed these rivers to be large, and he advised me to take tools along to make canoes, so that if we found the country so rough that we could not get along with our wagons we could descend one of those rivers to the Pacific.[6]

There was, of course, no such river. The Bartleson-Bidwell Party got lost on the Salt Lake desert and had to abandon their wagons. Three years later, in 1844, the Stevens Party would take wagons into California using the basic route discovered by the Bartleson-Bidwell Party.

Prior to the discovery of gold, the initial emigrant to California seems to have been motivated by a sense of adventure and perhaps of being overcrowded by settlers in the westernmost areas of the United States. Most were farmers who had heard of the land available near Sutter's Fort in the central valley of California. They were accustomed to moving as most had already emigrated to the edge of the country where the treeless prairies and Indian country began. They were, of course, influenced by the rumors of the perfect weather, the lack of disease, and the easy life promised to all who could settle there. John Bidwell recalls a conversation with a western Nebraska trading post operator, John Roubideaux:

Generally the first question which a Missourian asked about a country was whether there was any fever and ague. I remember his answer distinctly. He said there was but one man in California that has ever had a chill there, and it was a matter of so much wonderment to the people of Monterey that they went eighteen miles into the country to see him shake. Nothing could have been more satisfactory on the score of health. He said that the Spanish authorities were most friendly, and that the people were the most hospitable on the globe; that you could travel all over California and it would cost you nothing for horses or food. Even the Indians were friendly. His description of the country made it seem like a Paradise.[7]

The question about whether or not fever existed in California was motivated by a general outbreak of cholera in the U.S. during this period.

PLATE 1.

Supplies and Provisions

On your trip to California your selection of supplies is of the greatest importance. These supplies should be put up in the most secure, compact and portable shape. Bacon should be packed in strong sacks of a hundred pounds to each; or, in very hot climates, put in boxes and surrounded with bran, which, in a great measure, prevents the fat from melting away. If pork is used, in order to avoid transporting about forty percent of useless weight, it should be taken out of the barrels and packed like bacon; then so placed in the bottom of the wagons as to keep it cool. The pork, if well cured, will keep several months in this way, but bacon is preferable. Flour should be packed in stout double canvas sacks well sewed, a hundred pounds in each sack. Butter may be preserved by boiling it thoroughly and skimming off the scum as it rises to the top until it is quite clear like oil. It is then placed in tin canisters and soldered up. This mode of preserving butter has been adopted in the hot climate of southern Texas, and it is found to keep it sweet for a great length of time, and its flavor is but little impaired by the process. Sugar may be well secured in india-rubber sacks, or so placed in the wagon as not to risk getting wet. Dried vegetables are almost equal to the fresh, and are put up in such compact and portable form as easily to be transported over the plains. These dried vegetables are prepared by cutting them into thin slices and subjecting them to a very powerful press, which removes the juice and leaves a solid cake which, after having been thoroughly dried in an oven, becomes almost as hard as a rock. A small piece of this, about the size of a man's hand, when boiled swells up so as to fill a vegetable dish, and is sufficient for four men. Canned vegetables are very good, but not so portable as when put up in the other form.[8]

from The Prairie Traveler: A Handbook for Overland Expeditions, *1859*

Intersection of trail and State Highway 10, Kearney County, Nebraska.

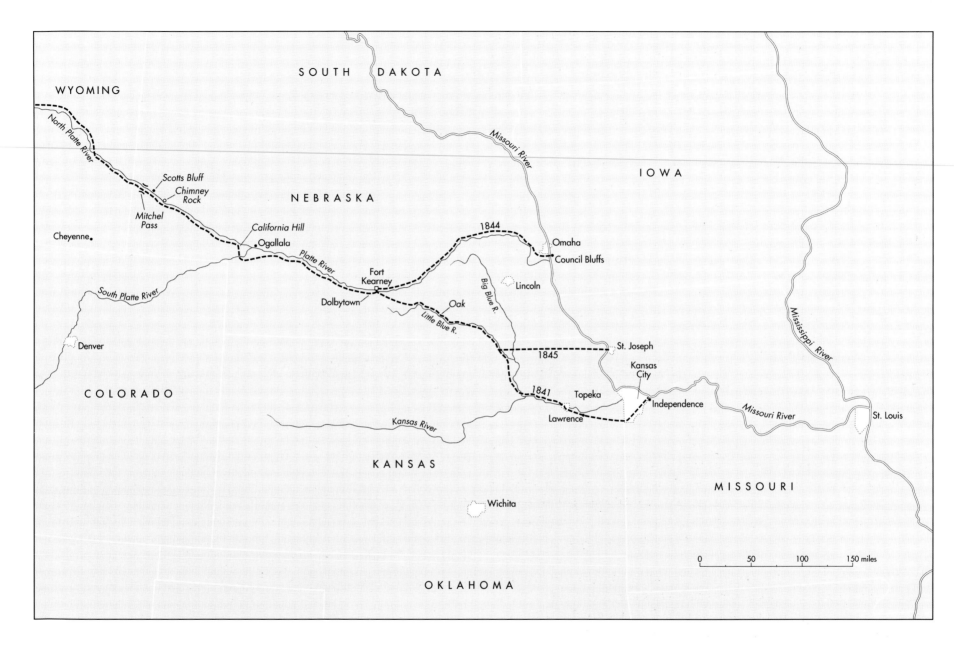

Map of the trail through Missouri, Kansas, and Nebraska.

The trip officially began in Saint Louis, Missouri, the gateway to the west, where steamboats would load passengers and belongings and travel upriver across the entire state of Missouri to Independence. At this point the trail would follow the Blue River through present-day Kansas City, Lawrence, Topeka, and Manhattan, Kansas, where it joined

THE MISSOURI, KANSAS, AND NEBRASKA CROSSING

the Little Blue River. The Little Blue headed northwest where the Platte River could be joined near Kearney, Nebraska. In general, this section of travel was not difficult, following rolling hills of the various river systems. There were, however, some very deep ravines and creeks that had to be crossed. Soon toll bridges appeared at the most difficult of these, which enabled wagons to cross more freely.

Once on the Platte and North Platte, the trail followed a 400-mile straight line route to Casper, Wyoming, on both sides of the river. This long haul up the Platte would have been simple if the river had been deep enough for riverboats. The river, however, did provide ample grass and water, but no trees for kindling wood. Instead, buffalo chips were used for fuel in cooking.

This section of trail went through the heart of the Great Plains area where enormous herds of buffalo still grazed. Their numbers would be greatly diminished in the late 1860s and 1870s as a systematic plan to eliminate the food supply of the Plains Indians was initiated. The emigrants of 1840–70, however, shot buffalo for both sport and the little meat that could be carried on already over-packed wagons.

The Plains Indians (Sioux and Pawnee) generally did not perceive the passing emigrants as a threat; they recognized that the travelers were interested in getting through as quickly as possible and not stopping to claim the local land for farms. Indians were ever-present, however; many times they camped around the various forts for trade purposes, were employed as scouts by the military, or were just plain curious. They were also seen along the trail, at river crossings, or riding alongside the wagons at discreet, or sometimes close distances, mostly looking.

The priority purchase for the trip west, after a wagon, was an adequate firearm. When first organized, most wagon trains were traveling arsenals; later, when they encountered difficult sections of trail and items had to be abandoned because of weight, extra rifles were among the items jettisoned. The presence of such firepower, however, gave confidence to emigrants when Indians came too close. Most Indian attacks occurred upon isolated travelers. Numbers found in recent research into Indian-caused deaths, rather than speculation by emigrants' accounts in diaries, reveal that only 127 deaths from 1840 to 1860 can be documented.

The first fort the emigrants encountered along the Platte was Fort Kearny in Nebraska; 350 miles later they came to Fort Laramie, then Fort Fetterman, and finally Fort Casper at 500 miles distance. They used these forts for minor repairs and limited resupply purchases, though in many cases the forts, too, were short on even basic provisions.

A young man that was with Uncle Stewart by the name of John Thomas accidentally shot himself with his six shooter. He was twirling it around and revolving it when it went off. The bullet went in on the right side through his breast and come out in his back on the same side. . . . Sad, sad fact, our friend died this evening between sundown and dark.[9]

Harriet Bunyard

PLATE 2.

Emigrants boarded riverboats in Saint Louis, Missouri, and traveled upriver 300 miles to this point near present-day Independence, Missouri. This was a busy landing site as the already established Santa Fe Trail also began here. A very steep section of the trail to begin with, it went through the concrete plant straight up the hillside onto the flat ledge on the left side of this scene. From there it followed along a ridge through Independence, passing about one block from the present-day Harry Truman Library.

This morning our boat started for the upper landing, which is twelve miles from the Lower.

We arrived about nine o'clock after a pleasant run of three hours. This landing has a hard appearance, being at the bottom of a very high bluff and close to the shore.

We landed the trunks and hired a man to take them to the city for 25 cents apiece while we walked, the distance being three miles. On arriving at the top of the hill, we had a grand view of the river below us. The road from the river to Independence runs through rolling woodland, which resembles our own forest at home. The oaks, hickory and other forest trees seemed like familiar friends. . . . The walk was a delightful one, and we relished it the more as were just freed from the confinement of the boat.

We arrived at Independence and took board at Mr. F. H. Hereford, Esq's house at $4 per week.[10]

Wiliam Swain, *May 3, 1849*

View of Independence Landing, beginning of trail, Independence, Missouri.

PLATE 3.   *Trail leaving Osage and Linden streets, Independence, Missouri.*

The depression in the grass at the middle of this photo is the trail remains known as a swale. The trail follows
the paved road in the background and continues out the bottom of this view and into a residential backyard.

PLATE 4.   *On Blue Ridge Blvd. at 59th Avenue, Raytown, Missouri.*

The cars are on the trail which is making its way through the large spread-out metropolis of Kansas City and most of its suburbs. The country is rolling hills in this area. Some traces of the trail remain when it crosses a river, or travels through a golf course. Otherwise it is under asphalt and housing development. In this area of Missouri the trail will follow the Big Blue River and its tributaries.

PLATE 5.

Organization of companies

After a particular route has been selected to make the journey across the plains, and the requisite number have arrived at the eastern terminus, their first business should be to organize themselves into a company and elect a commander. The company should be of sufficient magnitude to herd and guard animals, and for protection against Indians. From 50 to 70 men, properly armed and equipped, will be enough for these purposes, and any greater number only makes the movements of the party more cumbersome. In the selection of a captain, good judgement, integrity of purpose, and practical experience are the essential requisites. His duty should be to direct the order of march, the time of starting and halting, to select the camps, details and give orders to guards, and indeed, to control and superintend the movements of the company.

An obligation should then be drawn up and signed by all the members of the association, wherein each one should bind himself to abide in all cases by the orders and decisions of the captain, and to aid him by every means in his power in the execution of his duties; and they should also obligate themselves to aid each other, so as to the whole company. To insure this, a fund should be raised for the purchase of extra animals to supply the places of those which may give out or die on the road;

and if the wagon or team of a particular member should fail and have to be abandoned, the company should obligate themselves to transport his luggage. Thus it will be made the interest of every member of the company to watch-over and protect the property of others as well as his own. . . .

On long and arduous expeditions men are apt to become irritable and ill-natured, and oftentimes fancy they have more labor imposed upon them than their comrades, and that the person who directs the march is partial toward his favorites, etc. The man who exercises the greatest forebearance under such circumstances, who is cheerful, slow to take up quarrels, and endeavors to reconcile difficulties among his companions, is deserving of all praise, and will, without doubt, contribute largely to the success and comfort of an expedition. . . .

When a captain has once been chosen, he should be sustained in all his decisions unless he commit some manifesst outrage, at which time a majority of the company can remove him and put a better man in his place.[11]

from The Prairie Traveler: A Handbook for Overland Expeditions, *1859*

Trail enthusiast, near Rock Springs, Wyoming.

PLATE 6.

Fording Rivers

Many streams that the prairie traveler encounters are broad and shallow, and flow over beds of quicksand, which in seasons of high water, become boggy, and then are exceedingly difficult to cross. On arriving upon the bank of a river of this character which has not recently been crossed, the condition of the quicksand may be determined by sending an intelligent man over the fording-place, and, should the sand not yield under his feet, it may be regarded as safe for animals or wagons. Should it, however, prove soft and yielding, it must be thoroughly examined, and the best track selected. This can be done by a man on foot, who will take a number of sharp sticks long enough, when driven into the bottom of the river, to stand above the surface of the water. He starts from the shore, and with one of the sticks and his feet tries the bottom in the direction of the opposite bank until he finds the firmest ground, where he plants one of the sticks to mark the track. A man incurs no danger in walking over quicksand providing he step rapidly, and he will soon detect the safest ground. He then proceeds, planting his sticks as often as may be necessary to mark the way, until he reaches the opposite bank. The ford is thus determined, and if there are footmen in the party, they should cross before the animals and wagons, as they pack the sand, and make the track more firm and secure." [12]

from The Prairie Traveler: A Handbook for Overland Expeditions, *1859*

As we neared the spot where we designed to cross we observed at least 400 waggons on the bank and at least 3,000 oxen. . . . The shouting and hallooing combined with the bawling of cattle made a confusion of stunning sounds. . . .

The water was high and consequently we found it quite impossible to ford the river without swimming our horses as we rode them. . . . Ox teams . . . were thrown into confusion, some would become unyoked or get the chains over their backs instead of between them, and some would turn their heads in the wrong direction. The waggons would swing about in deep water. . . . Often they would be submerged, and their contents greatly injured, or they would upset and thus destroy all they contained, or float away to parts hitherto unexplored. [13]

Dr. Tompkins, *1850*

Crossing site of Big Blue River, Kansas City, Missouri.

PLATE 7. *The University of Kansas Football Stadium, Lawrence, Kansas.*

The trail goes through the stop sign and continues into the stadium on the right side. All the land in this area is farmed, and few traces of the original trail are visible. In places like this the route is pieced together from local historical records and USGS maps created in 1906.

PLATE 8. *McCanles Toll Bridge, Rock Creek Crossing, Jefferson County, Nebraska.*

In 1859 David McCanles constructed this toll bridge, which made crossing the steep-sided Rock Creek possible. The previous crossing site, a few hundred yards from here, was very treacherous. This was also the site of a Pony Express station and a stagecoach station in the 1850s. The structure in the background is a livestock building from that era with the trail passing in front. This area is currently a state park.

PLATE 9.

In this area of Nebraska the trail is following the shallow valley of the little Blue River in the general direction of the Platte River. The land is a combination of woods and cultivated farms. The trail through Oak, Nebraska, is well documented, and the local historian is a shopkeeper in the last store on the right with the flag outside. Along the Little Blue, just outside Oak, on August 7, 1864, Laura Roper, Mrs. William Eubanks, her four-year-old daughter, Belle, and baby son were captured by Cheyenne Indians. In 1929 Mrs. Roper returned to this area and identified the site, where a historical marker was placed. The wooden marker has subsequently decayed.

On the trail, looking west, Oak, Nebraska.

PLATE 10.

Red Vermillion Creek has perpendicular walls twenty-five feet deep on both sides. There was one difficult ford site. In 1848 Louis Vieux erected a toll bridge at the site of the bridge seen here, and charged $1 for the crossing. Vieux, originally from Chicago, raised his family here and made his living as a toll collector, business agent, and interpreter. His grave and his successive three wives graves are located on the bank of the creek. There are several other graves in the area. In 1849 a large group of emigrants camped here, and in less than a week fifty members died of asiatic cholera.

The large elm tree must have certainly witnessed all this as the old trail is underneath the road in this view. A plaque at its base reads:

Louis Vieux Elm Tree.
World Champion, 1985
U.S. Champion, 1979
Kansas Champion, 1978

It is officially the second largest American elm tree in the U.S. In 1992 it was struck by lightning and mostly destroyed.

This part of Kansas is known for enormously powerful thunderstorms of lightning and hail in the spring season, a time when most migrant traffic would be passing through.

Monday, May 16th Evening—We have had all kinds of weather today. This morning was dry, dusty and sandy. This afternoon it rained, hailed, and the wind was very high. Have been traveling all the afternoon in mud and water up to our hubs. Broke chains and stuck in the mud several times. The men and boys are all wet and muddy. Hard times but they say misery loves company. We are not alone on these bare plains, it is covered with cattle and wagons. . . .

Tuesday, May 17th We had a dreadful storm of rain and hail last night and very sharp lighting. It killed two oxen for one man. We have just encamped on a large flat prairie, when the storm commenced in all its fury and in two minutes after the cattle were taken from the wagons every brute was gone out of sight, cows, calves, horses, all gone before the storm like so many wild beasts. I never saw such a storm. The wind was so high I thought it would tear the wagons to pieces. Nothing but the stoutest covers could stand it. The rain beat into the wagons so that everything was wet, in less that 2 hours the water was a foot deep all over our camp grounds. As we could have no tents pitched, all had to crowd into the wagons and sleep in wet beds with their wet clothes on, without supper. The wind blew hard all night and this morning presents a dreary prospect surrounded by water, and our saddles have been soaking in it all night and are almost spoiled! . . .

Wednesday, June 1st It has been raining all day long and we have been traveling in it so as to be able to keep ahead of the large droves. The men and boys are all soaking wet and look sad and comfortless. (The little ones and myself are shut up in the wagons from the rain. Still it will find its way in and many things are wet; and take us all together we are a poor looking set, and all this for Oregon. I am thinking while I write, "Oh, Oregon, you must be a wonderful country." Came 18 miles today.)[14]

Amelia Stewart White, *1853*

Bridge at Red Vermillian Creek and prize-winning elm tree, Pottawatomie County, Kansas.

PLATE 11.

Dolbytown or Kearney City, located two miles west of Fort Kearney, was a cluster of about fifteen squalid adobe huts which housed the hangers-ons, dropouts, and marginal traders that often follow and crop up near military outposts. In a cornfield nearby is a historic marker indicating the site of Dirty Woman Ranch.

The Mormon Trail began at Council Bluffs, Iowa, and rapidly converged onto the Platte River near Fort Kearney. It is generally agreed that the Mormon trail kept to the north bank and the California-Oregon–bound travelers were on the south bank as Mormons were leary of mixing too closely with those they held responsible for murdering their prophet, Joseph Smith. However, both groups made many crossings, sometimes to avoid high water impasses or for resupply visits to forts, and to purchase suppplies from the independent traders who populated the route later in the migration. The long trudge up the Platte River begins at Fort Kearney.

We now come in sight of Fort Kearney and could see the glorious old "Star Spangled Banner" floating proudly on the breeze. The fort consists of about twenty houses occupied as barracks—officers quarters and a post office enclosing a square of about one acre with twelve six pounder guns mounted three on each side of the square. I saw—the commanding officer out riding with a fine rosy-looking lady who was also a good horsewoman; was told it was the famous Capt. May and his wife.

We were not allowed to stop in the immediate neighborhood of the "fort" the rules being strict that no one should camp within two miles. I stayed behind to get letters I found some from home the first I received since leaving . . . I read my letters found all well at home and then went out to the square to see the drill. There was two companies United States Regulars fine appearing men but sadly deficient of clothing. Almost every man was out at the knees or elbows. Even the officers looked shabby. I saw them trying to get gloves on which required a great deal of skill. They were full of holes and the fingers would not go out in the right place. However badly dressed they were they understood their drill perfectly. They were put through infantry and then another company through artillery drill. [15]

Tree Stumps at Kearney City Site, Nebraska.

PLATE 12.

These ruts are some of the few remaining in Nebraska.
They are a good example of trail which has not been
driven on since the late 1800s. Since most of Nebraska
is farmable, especially in the Platte River bottom, the
trail was long ago plowed up. These ruts have remained
because the hillside is far enough from the river to make
irrigation difficult. In 1988 OCTA (Oregon California
Trails Association) purchased the land in order to pre-
serve these ruts. At this section the trail is climbing a
hill after crossing the South Platte River and will soon
follow a ridge for twenty miles before descending to
follow the North Platte River. Crossing the South Platte
River was a dangerous affair, particularly during the
spring runoff .

Trail ascending from South Platte River crossing, California Hill, Keith County, Nebraska.

PLATE 13.

This was the first real hill of any consequence on the trail in nearly four hundred miles. The object of the descent was to reach the North Platte River. If not done here, one would have to make a seventeen-mile dry trek along the cliffs above the river for the next opportunity. Front and back wheels of the wagons were roped together to lock the wheels and then ropes were connected to people to hold back the wagons as they slid down the hill. The scar in the hillside and large gash in the earth mark the trail. The soil is so soft in this area that erosion has enlarged the trail into the gully in the foreground.

When travelers reached the North Platte River they followed it for almost three hundred miles with trails on both banks. The North Platte River had widths of a mile during spring runoff. Fortunately, it could usually be crossed by wading. As the river deepened, near Casper, Wyoming, private operators took people across on ferry boats.

We reach the brink of the hill near one-third of a mile high [Windlass Hill] which we have to descend to reach the level of the hollow. We detach all the oxen from the wagon except the wheel yoke, lock the the two hind wheels with the lock chain attached to the body of the wagon and wrap a log chain around the tire so it will cut into the ground when the wagon is in motion. Frequently the other five yokes of oxen are hitched with their heads to the wagon behind. They being unaccustomed to this treatment, pull back and help to slow down the wagon.

Everything in the front of the wagons must be tied securely, as out comes the goods when the descent is begun. I cannot say at what angle we descend but it is so great that some go as far as to say "the road hangs a little past the perpendicular!" [16]

Eroded ruts and Windlass Hill, Ash Hollow, Nebraska.

PLATE 14.

The North Platte River had one distinct difference: it was two miles wide and one foot deep and, compared to the torrid South Platte, had a placid current. The shallowness, typical of many western streams, was not obvious to emigrants whose knowledge was based upon eastern river characteristics.

One of our party, Robert Selfridge, more daring than the rest, proposed to swim over to the nearest island and bring a supply [of wood]. The river had every appearance of being a deep, as well as a broad and rapid stream; so Bob stripped off and most courageously plunged in, but so far from disappearing in the tide, he, naked as he was, walked all the way out to the island, without anywhere finding a depth of water half way up to his knees. His venture brought to the camp a good deal of amusement as well as sufficient fuel to cook our supper.[17]

Cornelius Cole

Broken guardrail, North Platte River, Lewellen, Nebraska.

PLATE 15.

Located just east of Scotts Bluff, Nebraska, Chimney
Rock could be seen three days in advance on the trail.
It is 300 feet from base to top and has eroded considerably in the past century compared to earlier drawings.
Made of loose clay interlaced with volcanic ash, it was
covered with the initials of passing emigrants. Many
diaries predicted it wouldn't last past a few years because it was so soft; the initials have mostly disappeared. Because emigrants were accustomed to the
flat landscape of the Midwest, they mentioned this
bizarre rock in every diary. To them it signaled the
beginning of the West. In 1992 it was struck by lightning and its height reduced by five feet. There is currently a movement to create a historical monument on
the site of this structure. It previously had no official
status.

*There is but one point, the southeastern where the em-
igrants can climb up the chimney, and every part of this
singular structure has names upon it, at the base and
even as high as thirty feet up the chimney. To accomplish this, men first cut places to put their feet, and then
cut places to hold by, and each venturesome climber
seems to wish to put his name above the last one. . . .
One poor fellow fell and was killed.*[18]

William Swain, *June 29, 1849*

Burning field near Chimney Rock, looking west, Morril County, Nebraska.

PLATE 16.   *On trail site, State Highway 92, approaching Mitchell Pass, Scotts Bluff, Nebraska.*

Mitchell Pass was opened in 1851 by the military and became the route of choice through this high rock area. In 1852 alone, 50,000 wagons passed. The ruts in the pass are cut eight feet into the sandstone because wagons had to travel single file. The trail intersects Highway 92 in the center of this photograph and continues under the pavement to the pass where it divides and is visible through the national monument located there.

Because of unpredictable rainfall, most of Wyoming is used for cattle grazing rather than plowed for crop planting. Consequently, much of the original trail still exists. This is in contrast to Nebraska where most of the trail has been farmed over.

Entering from the lower right side of the map, the trail follows both sides of the North

THE WYOMING CROSSING 4

Platte River through treeless grassland and rolling hills. Along this river it gradually ascends until it is 5,000 feet above sea level at Casper, Wyoming. Just west of Casper, at Independence Rock, the Sweetwater River will be joined and followed to the Continental Divide. This occurs at the south end of the Wind River Mountain range (a section of the Rockies) called South Pass, at 7,000 feet elevation. The ascent is gradual and the pass itself almost flat, an easy passage. Once over the pass, travelers encountered high desert terrain with several river crossings on the long down slope to Fort Bridger, Wyoming.

Unlike the previous forts along the trail, Fort Bridger was not a military establishment, but rather a resupply station. Although not exactly on the route to either California or Oregon, this fort had plentiful grass and water, good for fattening up traded, tired oxen for resale by the owner, Jim Bridger. After leaving Fort Bridger, the trail headed north towards Idaho to join the Bear River and to follow it around the north shore of the Great Salt Lake. A suitable south-shore crossing was never found for wagons, even though it would have been a much more direct route into California. The two trails to Oregon and California would remain the same until well into Idaho where they would eventually split. The Mormon Trail, however, split at Fort Bridger and headed over the Unita and Wasatch mountains, down Echo Canyon, and into Salt Lake City.

Emigrants who did not need to stop in Fort Bridger to rest or trade their livestock soon created the obvious shortcut after South Pass to join the Bear River. Both the Sublette and Dempsey-Hockenday cutoffs necessitated leaving river systems and traveling over a series of dry mountain divides, but the route was fifty miles less than going through Fort Bridger. The fort continued to service the Mormon emigration.

Although the terra firma in Wyoming was not particularly bothersome, the wind and water were. Powerful winds blow in the western half of the state, steady and toward the East, putting all but the lead wagon in stinging stirred-up dust. As a result, multiple trails were created as wagons spread out. Also, a wind chill factor, new to midwesterners and fresh Mormon recruits from England, would play its role in the high altitude, chilling rain, and sometimes early snows of Wyoming. Unlike the shallow, fordable South Platte

River, the North Platte and Green rivers simply could not be forded at high water times. The only solution for most was to pay the toll fees and wait in the long lines at the Mormon-operated ferry boat rafts.

Our manner of living is far preferable to any in the States. I never was so contented and happy before. Neither have I enjoyed such health for years. In the morning as soon as the day breaks the first that we hear is the words, "Arise! Arise!"—then the mules set up such a noise as you never heard, which puts the whole camp in motion. We encamp in a large ring, baggage and men, tents and wagons on the outside, and all the animals except the cows, which are fashioned to pickets, within the circle. . . . While the horses are feeding we get breakfast in a hurry and eat it. By this time the words, "Catch up! Catch up!" ring through the camp for moving. We are ready to start usually at six, travel till eleven, encamp, rest and feed, and start again about two; travel until six, or before, . . .

Tell mother I am a very good housekeeper on the prairie. I wish she could just take a peep at us while we are sitting at our meals. Our table is the ground, our tablecloth is an India-rubber cloth used when it rains as a cloak; our dishes are made of tin-basins for teacups, iron spoons and plates, for each of us, and several pans for milk and to put our meat in when we wish to set it on the table. Each one carries his own knife in his scabbard, and it is always ready to use. When the table things are spread, after making our own forks or sticks and helping ourselves to chairs, we gather around the table.

Husband always provides my seat, and in a way that you would laugh to see. It is the fashion of all this country to imitate the Turks. . . . We take a blanket and lay down by the table, and those whose joints will let them, follow the fashion; others take out some of the baggage (I suppose you know that there is no stones in this country, not a stone have I seen of any size on the prairie). For my part I fix myself as gracefully as I can, sometimes on a blanket, sometimes on a box, just as it is convenient. Let me assure you of this, we relish our food none the less for sitting on the ground while eating. We have tea and a plenty of milk, which is a luxury in this country.[19]

Narcissa Whiteman, *1843*

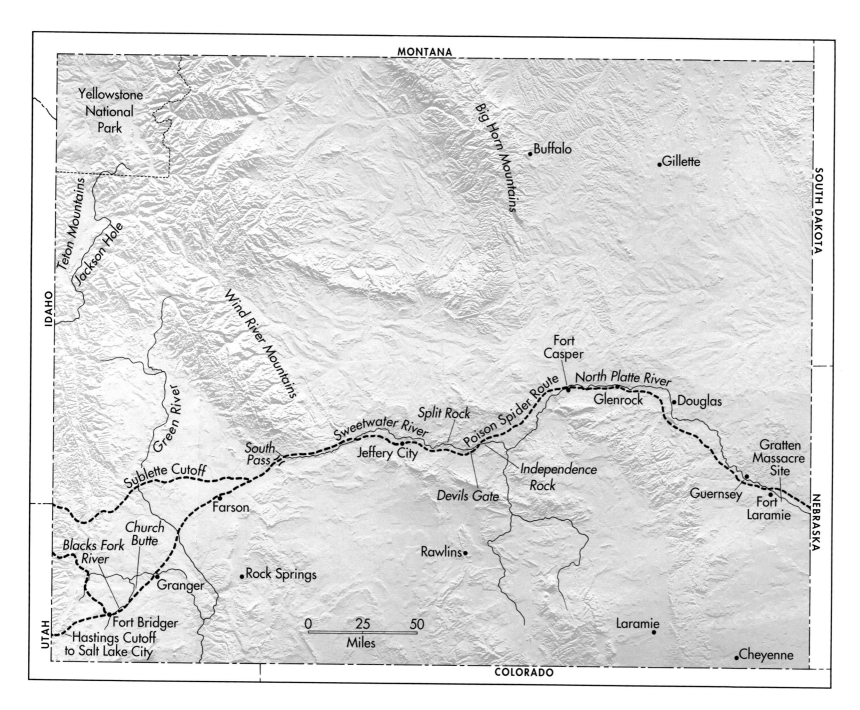

The trail across Wyoming.

PLATE 17.

Packing

In outfitting their wagons men are very prone to over-load their teams with a great variety of useless articles. It is a good rule to carry nothing more than is absolutely necessary for use upon the journey. One can not expect, with the limited allowance of transportation that emigrants usually have, to indulge in luxuries upon such expeditions, articles for use in California can be purchased there at less cost than that of overland transportation.

I would advise all persons who travel for any considerable time through a country where they can procure no vegetables to carry with them some essence of lemon as a prevention for scurvy.

The allowance of provisions for each grown person, to make the journey from the Missouri River to California, should suffice for 110 days. The following is deemed necessary; 150 lbs. of flour, or its equivalent in hard bread; 25 lbs. of bacon or pork, and enough fresh beef to be driven on the hoof to make up the meat component of the diet; 15 lbs. of coffee and 25 lbs. of sugar; also a quantity of yeast powders for making bread, and salt & pepper. These are the chief articles of subsistence necessary for the trip, and they should be used with economy, reserving a good portion for the western half of the journey. Heretofore many of the California emigrants have exhausted their stocks of provisions before reaching their journey's end, and have,
in many cases, been obliged to pay the most exorbitant prices in making up the deficiency. It is true that if persons choose to pass through Salt Lake City, and the Mormons happen to be in an amiable mood, supplies may sometimes be procured from them; but those who have visited them well know little reliance is to be placed upon their hospitality or spirit of accommodation.[20]

from The Prairie Traveler: A Handbook for Overland Expeditions, *1859*

It is worth noticing that on the Platte one may sometimes see the shattered wrecks of ancient claw-footed tables, well waxed and rubbed, or massive bureaus of carved oak. These, some of them no doubt the relics of ancestral prosperity in the colonial time, must have encountered strange vicissitudes. Brought, perhaps, originally from England; then, with the declining fortunes of their owners, borne across the Alleghenies to the wilderness of Ohio or Kentucky; then to Illinois or Missouri; and now at last fondly stowed away in the family wagon for the interminable journey to Oregon. But the stern privations of the way are little anticipated. The cherished relic is soon flung out to scorch and crack upon the hot prairie.[21]

Francis Parkman, *1849*

Banks of the North Platte River, Mitchell, Wyoming.

PLATE 18.   *Gratten Massacre site, near Lingle, Wyoming.*

The Gratten Massacre occurred on August 19, 1854, when 2nd Lieutenant John Gratten and twenty-nine soldiers attempted to arrest several Sioux Indians who had found and eaten a stray cow belonging to a Mormon emigrant. The inexperienced officer fired a cannon into an Indian lodge and fighting began. All the soldiers, Lt. Gratten, and a Brule Indian chief were killed. They were buried in a common grave here at the battlefield. The official marker placed in 1954 by the Historical Landmark Commission of Wyoming is in the far left of this view.

PLATE 19. *Hospital ruins, Fort Laramie, Wyoming.*

Four forts were constructed along the trail in Wyoming during the emigration to protect travelers from hostile Indians. The first years of the migrations saw few Indian problems except for minor theft. Not until after the 1860s, when the railroad was completed and land along the way was for sale for ranching and settlement, did problems escalate. A series of forts were built at the Laramie site. The first, Fort Henry, built in 1834, was a fur trading and supply center. The last fort, occupied by the military, was abandoned in 1890. One additional and historically valuable function they performed was to keep a count of the traffic passing through each year.

PLATE 20.

These ruts show the typical approach to ascending a
hill. They went straight up the fall line. The trail was
not a graded road, and any attempt to climb hills gently
along a contour line usually caused the wagons to tip
over. When this kind of ascent was unavoidable, however, ropes were connected on the uphill side of the
wagon. Several people walked along holding the ropes
to keep the wagon as vertical as possible. The usual
reason for climbing a hill like this would be to get to a
ridge which would then be the flattest route and provide long visibility. The river bottoms were used for
campsites because of their proximity to grass and water, but the trail was usually well away from the banks
since the water level changed so much during the season, thereby wiping out sections of trail during high
water.

Deep sandstone ruts near Guernsey, Wyoming.

PLATE 21.

How we do wish for some vegetables. I can really scent them cooking sometimes. I had an opportunity at noon to eat some of Mrs. Dobbins' cold beans. The boys cooked so much bacon with them that each bean had a rim of grease around it. Oh well, I can plainly see that I am too particular. But then one does like a change and about the only change we have from bread and bacon is to bacon and bread.

In respect to women's work the days are all very much the same except when we stop for a day. Then there is washing to be done and light bread to make and all kinds of odd jobs. Some women have very little help about camp being obliged to get the wood and water (as far as possible), make camp fires, unpack at night and pack up in the morning. . . . I am lucky in having a Yankee for a husband, so am well waited on.

Although there is not much to cook, the difficulty and inconvenience in doing it amounts to a great deal. So by the time one has squatted around the fire and cooked bread and bacon, made several trips to and from the wagon, washed the dishes (with no place to drain them) and gotten things ready for an early breakfast, some of the others already have their night caps on. At any rate, it is time to go to bed.

By the way, these buffalo chips, when well cured, are not at all offensive and make a very good substitute for wood.[22]

Helen Carpenter, *1849*

Eroded ruts and Laramie Peak, Platte County, Wyoming.

PLATE 22.

. . . to visit a remarkable mountain gorge—a natural bridge of solid rock, over a rapid torrent, the arch being regular as tho' shaped by art—30 feet from base to ceiling, and 50 to the top of the bridge—wild cliffs, 300 feet perpendicular beetled above us, and the noisy current swept along among huge fragments of rock at our feet. We had a dangerous descent, and forced our way through an almost impervious thicket, being compelled to take the bed of the stream in gaining a positon below. We call the water "Bridge Creek"![23]

Mathew C. Field, *July 12, 1843*

Ayers Natural Bridge, near LePrele Reservoir, Wyoming.

PLATE 23.

Alva Unthank is believed to have died of cholera or dysentery. The date on the headstone reads July 2, 1850. One week earlier he had carved his initials on Register Cliff, where they are still visible. Most emigrants were not buried with this much care. This particular grave has both headstone and footstone with carvings on both. A more typical grave was a shallow trench about eighteen inches deep, covered with a single layer of random rocks, no inscriptions. Another common technique was to bury the dead on the trail without a rock covering and drive the wagons over the site to confuse the scent in order to keep coyotes and wolves from digging up the body. This had mixed success as many diaries comment on seeing scattered limbs and freshly opened graves along the trail.

There was a general outbreak of cholera in the United States during this time, and it was intensified on the trail because of unsanitary water. The disease struck quickly; a person could show the first symptoms in the morning and be dead by nightfall. The bacteria count in water holes was high because they were used by animals and humans alike, with seemingly no regard for those who followed. The county road in this view is the trail.

David Ayers, one of our company, puked and purged all night and upon examining his condition this morning found he had the cholera, as much so as any case I ever saw. All the symptoms were present even to the rice water discharges. I went to work with him faithfully, he lying in his wagon while we were moving on, and now he is very much better, circulation restored, discharges altered, etc. I placed a mustard plaster over his stomach and administered Davis pain killer in large quantities, at the same time making him inhale and perspire large draughts of fresh air, etc.[24]

Addison Crane, *1852*

Cholera was prevalent on the plains at this time; the train preceding as well as the one following ours had one or more deaths, but fortunately we had not a single case of the disease. Often several graves together stood as silent proof of smallpox or cholera epidemic. The Indians spread the disease among themselves by digging up the bodies of the victims for the clothing. The majority of the Indians were badly pock-marked. . . .[25]

Catherine Haun, *1849*

Emigrant grave and power plant, Douglas County, Wyoming.

PLATE 24. *On the trail, Evansville, Wyoming.*

Until 1992, the California-Oregon Trail did not have any federal protection. Any safeguarding, marking, or preservation was done on a voluntary basis by civic and historical groups and by ranchers who valued the remaining traces through their property. In this view the trail meanders through the Texaco Oil refinery and continues out the bottom of the photograph under the railroad tracks. In the summer of 1992, Congress passed legislation declaring it a national historic trail.

PLATE 25. *Bessemer Bend crossing site, North Platte River, Wyoming.*

Bessemer Bend is located just west of Casper, Wyoming, and is the last crossing of the North Platte River. The river takes a sharp turn south, here in the wrong direction. At this point all trails—Mormon, California, and Oregon—become one. A fifty-mile route to the next river system begins here. The next river, the Sweetwater, leads to the Continental Divide. At this crossing the trail is about one mile above sea level. However, the route to this point was such a gentle uphill that it seemed flat. The trail forded the river at the same location as the iron grate.

PLATE 26.

The trail follows along the base of this ridge on the left side and heads overland for about forty miles to join the Sweetwater River. This section of trail is high desert and sagebrush. Rocky Ridge forms a narrow gorge squeezing the trail through a small passage which was, until recently, a one-lane dirt road. About ten years ago it was blasted open to create a wider oil-pumping-station service road. This ridge has a large number of emigrant names carved into and painted on stone.

Clothing

A suitable dress for prairie traveling is of great importance to health and comfort. Cotton or linen fabrics do not sufficiently protect the body against the direct rays of the sun at midday; nor against rains or sudden changes of temperature. Wool, being a nonconductor, is the best material for this mode of locomotion, and should always be adopted for the plains. The coat should be short and stout, the shirt of red or blue flannel, such as can be found in almost all the shops on the frontier; this, in warm weather, answers for an outside garment. The pants should be of thick soft woolen material, and it is well to have them re-enforced on the inside, where they come in contact with the saddle, with soft buckskin, which makes them more durable and comfortable. Woolen socks and stout boots, coming up well at the knees, and made large, so as to admit the pants, will be found the best for horsemen, and they guard against rattlesnake bites.

In traveling through deep snow during very cold weather in winter, moccasins are preferable to boots or shoes, as being more pliable, and allowing a freer circulation of the blood. To repair shoes an awl with buckskin strings is used. They should never be forgotten in making up the outfit for a prairie expedition.[26]

from The Prairie Traveler: A Handbook for Overland Expeditions, *1859*

While traveling, mother was particular about Louvina and me wearing sunbonnets and long mitts in order to protect our complexions, hair and hands. Much of the time I should like to have gone without that long bonnet poking out over my face, but mother pointed out to me some girls who did not wear bonnets and as I did not want to look as they did, I stuck to my bonnet finally growing used to it.[27]

Adrietta Hixon

Tour group searching for emigrant names, Poison Spider route, Natrona County, Wyoming.

PLATE 27.

Independence Rock is a turtle-shaped granite rock, 200 feet high and ¼ mile long. It looms above a high desert region, which is flat to this point. Its name reflects its importance as a milestone along the trail. If reached by July Fourth, emigrants knew they were on schedule to arrive in California before the Sierra snows began. The entire surface of this rock is peppered with graffiti which shows clearly today. The Sweetwater River was joined here and so it was a major campsite, giving all ample time to add their initials to its surface.

I went to the rock for the purpose of recording my name with the swollen catalog of others traced upon its sides; but having glanced over the strange medley, I became disgusted, and, turning away, resolved, "If there remins no other mode of immortalizing myself, I will be content to descend to the grave unhonored and unsung!"[28]

Rufus B. Sage, *1842*

"Milo J. Ayer, age twenty-nine 1849" graffiti. View from the top of Independence Rock, Wyoming.

PLATE 28.

The immensely powerful wind that existed on the prairies was a bane for emigrants. Almost always from the west, it slowed wagons' forward progress, created blinding dust for trailing wagons, and inspired a mind-numbing stupor in those walking against it, which was everyone except the wagon drivers.

During the 1859–60 Pikes Peak gold rush in Colorado, those same winds would be an inspiration for a new invention: "the Prairie Ship." This device was a wagon with sail attached and was intended to get gold miners to the fields faster than conventional methods. It used no draft animals. Several different prototypes were made and "sailed," one having a hand-crank mechanism inside that turned the wheels in case of no wind. One actually made it from Independence to Denver by following the emigrant trail up the Platte River and then diverting along the South Platte to Colorado. The invention never caught on in any practical sense.

The maiden voyage of the *Pepper Wind Wagon*, named after its inventor, was described in the *Kansas Weekly Herald* in 1860 as follows:

> *"…everything worked to a charm. The occupants gliding swiftly over the prairies, were delighting themselves with anticipation of a speedy and comfortable trip to the mines, when the velocity of the vehicle created a lively alarm for their safety. The wagon sped onward before the driving wind, faster and faster yet, until the axeltrees broke and deposited them all upon the ground, in a somewhat damaged condition from broken heads, bruised limbs and bodies. The speed of the machine is said to have been forty miles per hour. We suggest the use of brakes."* [29]

Strong wind and video man, Independence Rock, Wyoming.

PLATE 29.

Devil's Gate is located just eight miles from Independence Rock. The Sweetwater River cuts through this gorge, but the trail could not follow. Instead, it took a short detour around. Almost all who passed took the brief walk off the trail to peer into this 500-foot-deep gap. The area has several graves and migrant names cut into the rocks. All diaries mention this site.

. . . Visited the Devils Gate the most noted curiosity along this road. This is indeed wonderful to look at and one stands in awe of Him Who tore asunder the mountains and holds the winds in the hollow of his hands. But why attempt a description. All I could say would not add up to the sublimity of the scene. It speaks for itself.[30]

Martha Missouri Moore, July 23, 1860

Devil's Gate, Natrona County, Wyoming.

PLATE 30.

On this peaceful creek bank sixty-seven members of
the James G. Willie Company froze to death in 1856.
This was a Mormon handcart company bound for Salt
Lake. The handcart, usually provided by the Mormon
Church, was used by emigrants who could not afford to
purchase wagons and draft animals. It was pushed and
pulled by hand. Many early Mormon emigrants were
inexperienced converts from England who were not
accustomed to western travel and weather. This particular company decided to begin the trip, over the objec-
tions of the captain, even though they got a late start.
Of the 404 in the company, 77 died of exposure when
heavy snows started in October. In general, the
Mormon migration had a highly organized structure
from the recruiting end of the East Coast and Europe,
to the church-sponsored relay teams that would leave
Salt Lake and meet the companies with fresh supplies
on the trail. The saga and history of that migration hold
an important place in Mormon tradition. The California
and Oregon travelers, in contrast, were left to their own
resources and had about twice the distance to go.

Rock Creek campground, site of Mormon handcart disaster, Fremont County, Wyoming.

PLATE 31.

The Sweetwater River, named after a good-tasting water, has its headwaters in the distant mountain range. It flows in a gentle meandering fashion down from the high plateau. Following the road seen in this view, the trail passes through the Continental Divide at a low spot in the distant Wind River mountain range, about forty miles away. Along the rocky right side of this view, about two miles farther up the river, members of the Mormon handcart company led by Martin perished in the winter of 1856. The Martin company was following a few days behind the Willie company. They made several mistakes, including throwing away a hundred buffalo robes left for them at Fort Laramie because they were too heavy, and wading across the freezing North Platte River because they wanted to save the ferry crossing fee. The site, called Martins Cove, has a historic marker placed by the Mormon Church. It is estimated that up to 150 emigrants perished in the Martin company. The following accounts were given by members of a rescue team sent out by Brigham Young from Salt City to meet both the Willie and Martin companies.

. . . Many of the immigrants whose extremities were frozen, lost their limbs, either whole or in part. Many such I washed with water and Castile soap, until the frozen parts would fall off, after which I would sever the limb with my scissors. Some of the emigrants lost toes, others fingers, and again others whole hands and feet. . . .

Ephraim Hanks, *1856*

. . . A condition of distress here met my eyes that I never saw before or since. The train was strung out for three or four miles. There were old men pulling and tugging their carts, sometimes loaded with a sick wife or children—women pulling along sick husbands—little children six to eight years old struggling through the mud and snow. As night came on the mud would freeze on their clothes and feet. There were two of us and hundreds needing help. What could we do?"[31]

Dan Jones, *1856*

View of meandering Sweetwater River and Tom Sun Ranch, looking west.

PLATE 32.

We are hardly half way. I felt tired & weary. O the luxury of a house, a house! I felt what some one expressed who had traveled this long & tedious journey, that, "it tries the soul." I would have given all my interest in California, to have been seated around my own fireside surrounded by friend & relation. That this journey is tiresome, no one will doubt, that it is perilous, the deaths of many testify, and the heart has a thousand misgivings & the mind is tortured with anxiety, & often as I passed the fresh made graves, I have glanced at the side boards of the waggon, not knowing how soon it might serve as a coffin for some one of us; but thanks for the kind care of Providence we were favored more than some others.[32]

Lodisa Frizzell, *1852*

Trail exit from uranium mine tailings dust storm, near Jeffery City, Wyoming.

PLATE 33.

South Pass, the Continental Divide on the trail in Wyoming, was discovered in 1812 by trappers heading east from Astoria, Oregon. The land is almost flat here, and the original trail was five or six ruts wide. Ezra Meeker carved the large marker in the foreground in 1906. He had traveled west as an emigrant fifty-six years earlier and made this return trip with a mule-drawn wagon to promote and popularize the trail. The distant marker, placed in 1916, reads "Narcissa Prentiss Whitman, Elizabeth Spalding. First white women to cross this pass, July 4, 1836." Narcissa and her husband, Dr. Marcus Whitman, were killed in the 1847 massacre at their medical mission in Walla Walla, Washington. Eighteen-year-old Nancy Kelsey was the first California-bound woman to pass here in 1841. She was the only woman among the thirty-three members of the Bartleson-Bidwell party.

South Pass summit, Continental Divide, looking west, Wind River Mountains, Wyoming.

PLATE 34.

After crossing South Pass, the original trail headed
in a general out-of-the-way direction southward to Fort
Bridger. Soon, shortcuts or cutoffs were created in a
direct line west toward California and Oregon. In spite
of Jim Bridger's efforts, motivated by lost trade, these
new routes flourished even though they traveled
through dry mountainous country. In this photograph,
the trail descended the bluffs in the distance and then
crossed the Green River by Mormon toll ferry. It then
crossed the highway and climbed the hill through the
center of this photograph. The people below are examining the cliff face, which contains hundreds of emigrant names.

*Before we reached the river, our cattle became aware that
we were nearing water and showed signs of great impatience.
. . . When the stream was actually in sight, we found it necessary to unyoke the teams and let them loose to prevent them
from stampeding with the wagons. The approach was down
quite a steep mountainside. As soon as they were free, they
rushed pell-mell down into the river. It was a beautiful, clear
stream, and they stood in it drinking and cooling their feet
for a long time. It required a good deal of urging to get them
out, drive them up the hills, and reyoke them.*[33]

William Swain, *1849*

Green River crossing site, La Barge, Wyoming, on Sublette Cutoff.

PLATE 35.

I would make a brave effort to be cheerful and patient until the camp work was done. Then starting out ahead of the team and my men folks, when I thought I had gone beyond hearing distance, I would throw myself down on the unfriendly desert and give way like a child to sobs and tears, wishing myself back home with my friends and chiding myself for consenting to take this wild goose chase.[34]

Lavinia Porter

Coyote on sand, car on trail, Blue Point, Wyoming.

PLATE 36.

After the mid-1850s, most of the travel on this section of trail was Mormon emigration. The Unita Mountain Range is in the background and due west of them is the Great Salt Lake Valley. The cliff from which the view was made is carved with emigrant and contemporary names, among them a misspelled Brigam Young. This section of trail is headed for Fort Bridger about ten miles distant. Fort Bridger was an early trading post. Utah president Brigham Young purchased it in 1853, and it became an important resupply station for Mormons. The trail follows the Blacks Fork River here which will soon open up to a large grassy meadow, the site of Fort Bridger.

At the time of the breaking out of the gold excitement in California, Bridger made a big strike by selling the little necessaries of life to the travelers, as they passed by in 1850, '51 and '52; the emigration across was very large, and after leaving the Missouri River there was a stretch of about 1000 miles, so by the time they got to his place they were all pretty tired, and their stock in many instances very footsore. . . . Bridger would trade their worn out stock for about one tenth what they were worth, and the stock, after a little rest, would come out fat in about two months. A lame or worn-out steer in that country was worth about $1.50, and oftentimes the people could not get away on account of their cattle being so low. After the rush to California overland died away, the Mormon emigration kept him up for years. Then in 1857 when the Mormon War started, our troops were encamped in his midst, and that was also a harvest for him. Albert Sidney Johnston, the commander of the Expedition, rented the fort of him, and made a reserve there of 12 miles square, and put up very good log quarters for the troops, and since then, [it] has always been kept as a military post.[35]

Richard Thomas Akley, *1858*

View from Names Rock, trail terminating in ranch house, near Lyman, Wyoming, approaching Fort Bridger.

PLATE 37.

At Fort Bridger one could take the perilous Hastings Cutoff to California. J. Lansford Hastings, who had traveled it by horse, promoted the cutoff and claimed it was a shorter route. It crossed the southern end of the Great Salt lake and was never suitable for wagon travel because of the soft, sinky crust surface of the salt flats and the immense distance for oxen between water sources—eighty miles. Hastings published a guidebook extolling its values, too early in the migration period for the truth to be known. Jim Bridger encouraged the cutoff to keep emigrant travel passing through his fort, even though he never traveled it himself. The Donner-Reed party of 1846 decided to follow it. In doing so they lost two months travel time and got trapped in the winter snows of the Sierra in California, resulting in the well-known tragedy.

They got a late start, and the main group of sixty wagons began with Hastings as leader. Never catching up, they followed notes and tracks left by Hastings along the way. They got lost in the Wasatch Mountains east of Salt Lake, only making one mile per day struggling down Emigration Canyon into Salt Lake, as they hacked their way through river bottom saplings. One year later, in 1847, Brigham Young would use the trail the Donner Party broke through the Wasatch Range to lead his people, for the first time, into the Salt Lake Valley.

Mr. Bridger informs me that the route we design to take, is a fine level road, with a plenty of water and grass, with the exception before stated. It is estimated that 700 miles will take us to Capt. Sutter's Fort, which we hope to make in seven weeks from this day.

[There] is said to be a saving of 350 or 400 miles in going to California, and a better route. We are now only 100 miles from the Great Salt Lake by the new route—in all 250 miles from California; while by way of Fort Hall it is 650 or 700 miles—making a great saving in favor of jaded oxen and dust. On the new route we will not have dust, since there are but 60 wagons ahead of us.[36]

James Reed, 1846

My impressions are unfavorable to the route, especially for wagons and families; but a number of the emigrant parties now encamped here have determined to adopt it, with Messrs. Hastings and Hudspeth as their guides; and are now waiting for some of the rear parties to come up and join them.[37]

Edwin Bryant, 1846

Parade grounds, Fort Bridger, Wyoming.

PLATE 38.

This cutoff, a variation of the Sublette Cutoff, is headed
toward the Bear River Valley system. The trail in this
section passes over high plateau and treeless mountains and its direction being influenced by where water
could be found and where the divide passes were located. This section is working its way toward Pine Tree
Campground, a year-round spring located at the base
of the distant mountains. Cutoffs such as this, almost
by definition, meant leaving a river system, and instead
traveling a waterless overland route. Occasionally, the
springs along the way would be dry and the quality of
the water was severely compromised. Giardia and dysentery were usually the result of drinking this water.

*Once we came to a puddle where rain water had been
standing til green on top and so muddy that if their had
been a hog about, I should have set it down as one of
their wallowing places. Yet this stuff which would have
been rejected very suddenly by my stomach at home, I
drank with considerable relish by shutting my eyes and
holding my breath. This is what is called seeing one of
the elephant's tracks.*[38]

Elisha D. Perkins, *1856*

"To see the Elephant" was a common phrase
of the emigrant period and referred to experi-
encing something in its extreme—in this case,
the trip west.

Car caravan on Dempsey Cutoff, Lincoln County, Wyoming.

PLATE 39.   *Descent of Dempsey Cutoff into the Bear River Valley, Wyoming-Idaho border.*

PLATE 40.   *Trail site through Bear River Valley, Idaho.*

The Bear River system drains off the high plateau and northwest around the Wasatch mountain range, eventually emptying into the Great Salt Lake. The trail passes north of the lake. This northwest direction was convenient for Oregon travelers but not for California emigrants. However, there was no choice as the routes through the Wasatch range and across the southern end of the Great Salt Lake were not practical for wagons. By this time all trails and cutoffs are in the valley floor and beneath the highway, which travels down the Bear River in this view.

PLATE 41.

Soda Springs was a source of wonder for travelers. There were several springs in the area which produced natural carbonated water. Emigrants would mix sugar with the water, along with flavoring, to create a soft drink. Most of the springs are now under the Alexander Reservoir, seen on the right of this view.

One of our company, R. L. Doyle, made a wager that he could stop the flow of water from this spring by sitting on the crevice. He did not have to wait very long for the flow, it came gradually at first, but increased in force every moment. Doyle soon began bobbing up and down at a fearful rate. At this stage of the fun several of the boys took hold of Doyle and tried to hold him on the crevice, but in this they failed, for the more weight they added to Doyle the more power the spring seemed to have, and Doyle kept on bobbing up and down like a cork. Finally Doyle cried out, "Boys there's no use trying to hold the Devil down. It can't be did. I am now pounded into a beefsteak." [39]

Enoch Conyers, *1852*

Trail depression through fourteenth fairway, Soda Springs Golf Course,

PLATE 42.

At this significant spot on a grassy bank overlooking the Raft River in Idaho, the California and Oregon trails will separate. Oregon travelers will continue to follow the Snake River into the northwest, whereas the California emigrants will begin a 150-mile trek, jumping from one small creek to another until they join the Humboldt. The Oregon trace leaves the lower left and the California trace the lower right side in the view.

Over the years much of the trail has been marked. No single group or organization has covered its entire length. Boy Scout troops, the Mormon Church, the Bureau of Land Management, U.S. Park Service, Trails West Association, Oregon California Trails Association, and local Rotary Clubs are just some of those who have placed markers and plaques along its length. Consequently, there is a large variety of trail markers. The concrete markers seen in the background have been placed by the Bureau of Land Management. Since they are concrete, they are easily destroyed by bullets and tipped over by cattle using them for scratching poles in a treeless landscape. Recently, a flexible plastic marker has been substituted. The Trails West Association, headquartered in Reno, Nevada, tried to minimize vandalism by constructing markers of railroad rail steel, welded into a T-shape and potted into concrete in the soil. This was to keep four-wheel-drive enthusiasts from winching them out. A bronze plaque with words was riveted to the cross-T. Often the bronze plaque is stolen.

July 17. We then struck off more nearly to the south, while the creek ran due west. We noticed at this point where some persons, and supposed them to be emigrants, had set fire to the grass either by design or accident, and it burnt for several miles on the side of the road and was still burning. If it was done by design it was unpardonable. They should certainly think those who are coming behind them. Six miles of dust, in clouds, thick and impalpable, brought us again to the same Cachia Creek [Raft River] now running due south. We encamped in its valley, with good grass, wood and water, and no mosquitoes. In fact, this was the prettiest encampment since leaving the Platte. Here goes off the last road to Oregon, taking directly over the bluffs.

July 18. The morning broke clear, beautiful, and refreshing. After a good cup of coffee we were off again with spirits buoyant as air.[40]

Wakeman Bryarly, *1849*

May 13 . . . Henry has been no better to day. Soon after we stopped to night a man came along with a wheel barrow going to California he is a dutchmann He wheels his provisions and clothing all day and then stops where night overtakes him sleeps on the ground in the open air He eats raw meat and bread for his supper I think that he will get tired wheeling his way through the world by the time he gets to California.[41]

Lydia Allen Ruud, *1852*

David Eagle at the Split of the California and Oregon trails, Raft River, Idaho.

PLATE 43.

The Hudspeth Cutoff passes from left to right beneath the watering machine. It was a supposed shortcut 100 miles long, used primarily by anxious 49er gold seekers either on foot or muleback, and not by wagons. This type of watering has erased large sections of trail since its invention. A water well is drilled beneath them and the water distributed from the well and along the length of the machine through pipes. The entire machine then moves either in a giant circle or a straight line sprinkling as it goes. When the well runs dry, the area is abandoned, and the machine moved to a new location. Most agreed that the Hudspeth Cutoff saved little time and not much distance.

We had been told and had seen notes and cards stating the same thing that it was 100 miles to Humboldt River from the commencement of this cut off. As we had travelled that distance on it we were in hopes today to see that famous river and camp on its banks tonight. . . . Judge our disappointment and heartsinking to learn after a hard morning's travelling on reaching "the row of trees" that we were on the head of the Raft River, and that it was 130 miles yet to the Humboldt! . . . It took us sometime to reconcile ourselves to being thus "set back" in our calculations and we began to believe that this is indeed a long road and almost endless . . . camped . . . directly opposite where the Fort Hall road coming down the hill unites with the cut-off.[42]

Elisha D. Perkins, *1849*

Sprinkling machine on trail, Hudspeth Cutoff, near Malta, Idaho.

PLATE 44.

Having arrived in California, not all stayed to join the gold rush or try ranching or farming in the Central Valley. Many had remembered the fertile river valleys along the trail and their potential for cattle grazing or farming. The primary factor in settling this land was how long it took to remove any Indian threat. Once this was done, by the end of the 1870s, backtracking and settlement would begin. Emigrants of certain national origins favored certain areas, just as they did in the first migration to the Midwest. For instance, large numbers of Basque settled in Nevada for its sheep-raising potential, and Scandinavians claimed the Platte River environs for its rich farmland. The pioneer cabin in the photograph is the remains of an early attempt to settle in the upper reaches of Cassia Creek, today still a well-watered grazing and agriculture area. The telephone poles in this view follow the trail up over Elba Pass, Idaho, seen in the background.

Saturday, August 23 . . . Oh dear, I do so want to get there. It is now almost four months since we have slept in a house. If I could only be set down at home with all the folks I think there would be some talking as well as resting. Albert is so very miserable too, that I don't enjoy myself as well as I would if he was well. There have been Indians around today begging. We are glad to see them do so now, for all we are disgusted with the wretched creatures. [43]

Jane Gould Tortillott, *1862*

Pioneer cabin, approaching Elba Pass, Idaho.

PLATE 45.

Entry into this scenic valley is through the low spot in the center. Most emigrant diaries agree that this was more fascinating than any previous campground. The valley is filled with the type monolith shown here and is a popular rock-climbing area today. The granite structures seen here are about thirty feet high, many having emigrant names carved into them. A trail existed between Salt Lake City and this campsite. Mormon traders used this route to meet California-bound emigrants, for exchange of information and goods.

Almo, Idaho, is located near the entrance to the valley and was the reported scene of the greatest massacre of emigrants in the trail's twenty-year history.

In the town school yard is a stone monument which reads:

ALMO IDAHO
DEDICATED TO THE MEMORY
OF THOSE WHO LOST THEIR LIVES IN A
HORRIBLE INDIAN MASSACRE 1861
THREE HUNDRED IMMIGRANTS WESTBOUND
ONLY FIVE ESCAPED
ERECTED BY S & D [SONS AND DAUGHTERS]
  OF IDAHO PIONEERS
1938

No other massacre of emigrants exceeded twenty deaths. According to an old Shoshone Indian version, the bodies were buried in the trenches dug under several of the wagons for protection during the several-day siege. No bodies nor any remains of more than

Aug. 29. We entered a very extraordinary valley, called the "CITY OF CASTLES."... A couple of miles long, and probably ½ mile broad. A light grey decripitating granite, (probably altered by fire) in blocks of every size, from that of a barrel to the dimensions of a large dwelling-house; groups, Masses on Masses, and Cliffs; and worn, by the action of ages of elementary affluences, into strange and romantic forms.—The travellers had marked several large blocks, as their fancy dictated the resemblance to houses, castles, &c.—On one was marked (with tar) "NAPOLEON'S CASTLE," another "CITY HOTEL," &c. We nooned among these curious monuments of nature. I dined hastily, on bread and water and while others rested, I explored and sketched some of these queer rocks. A group, on left of the trails, resembled gigantic fungii, petrified, other clusters were worn in cells and caverns; and one, which contrasted with the size and height of the adjacent rocks, seemed no larger than a big chest, was, to my astonishment, when close to it, quite large, hollow, with an arched entrance, and capable of containing a dozen persons.... This, from its peculiar shape, I named the "Sarcophagus Rock." While nooning, 2 Mormon young men, on horses, with Mexican equipment, came up; said they were trading for broken-down cattle, and had a camp and wagon not far off, in a small valley ... on desiring some information, one of them took out of his pocket a sort of Guide book, formed of a sheet of paper folded small, miserably written, and worse spelling, which he said was the last he had, and I might take it for 50¢, but that he had sold a number, to the emigrants for $1 each. I purchased it more for curiosity than any idea of its serving me en route. I have discovered no sign of my train having passed here, and conclude that they are ahead, yet must have passed through this valley. Left my card in Sacophagus Rock.[44]

J. Goldsborough Bruff, *1849*

sixty wagons were ever found. Furthermore, there is no record of military retaliation, no mention in the newspapers of the time—the *Salt Lake Desert News* and the Sacramento or San Francisco papers. The Indian agents from the area filed no record in Washington, D.C. In spite of this, the massacre is mentioned in history books on southeast Idaho. Current theory is that the event never happened but was a hoax created to stimulate tourism and attention to the City of Rocks area.

Granite monoliths in City of Rocks campground, near Almo, Idaho.

PLATE 46.

The route came straight through the Wasatch range
(seen in the background) and then south of the Great
Salt Lake across the salt flats, an eighty-mile waterless
desert. The route next took a severe detour south to
circumnavigate the Ruby Mountains before finally joining the main trail near present-day Elko, Nevada. Parts
of the cutoff were used later by impatient gold seekers
traveling faster on foot or horseback. The trail was
most likely under the highway in this photograph, as
the road is pinched into a narrow passage between the
mountains on the right and the Great Salt Lake on the
left in this view.

On Hastings Cutoff, looking east, Magma, Utah.

PLATE 47.

The trail passes from right to left through this view somewhere in front of the distant mountains. In 1846 four wagons were abandoned by the Donner-Reed party on this playa when their draft animals died. Over the years the site was visited by souvenir hunters and historians alike and most of the remains of the wagons removed. In the 1980s high water levels in the Great Salt Lake were near flood stage and it was decided to pump water into the playa where the wagons were. The National Historic Preservations Act of 1966 allowed a final excavation before pumping could begin. This excavation was carried out by the Utah State Historical Society which removed all remaining material to ground level and below during 1983 to 1988.

At this encampment, I have conversed with a number of men who have just come through by way of Hastings' Cut-Off, or rather "Cut-On," as they term it, and they give it as their opinion, that it is a longer route than the northern one by more than fifty miles. They had to cross a desert, ninety miles, without grass or water. It is a level, salt desert, and lies contiguous to the great Salt Lake. It seems to be a dangerous road to travel, especially towards the western limit. If caught upon this part of it in a shower of rain, the consequence would be disasterous, if not fatal; particularly as to the wagons and animals; all would sink, to rise no more. The road runs upon a crust, of no great thickness, covering an ocean of mud, saturated with salt. A small amount of rain dissolves this crust, and leaves the traveler in a most perilous situation. Many teams have been lost in this dreary plain. In dry weather the desert can be crossed without danger of sinking. Let all travelers entirely avoid this route; there has been inexpressible suffering upon it the present season for want of water. Hundreds must have perished of thirst, had not some teams after they had crossed, returned loaded with casks of water, for the relief of the famishing multitudes.[45]

Franklin Langworthy, *1850*

The Mormans recommended the emigrants on the Hastings Cutoff to take no more than 20 days provisions as that would be ample to take them to the mines. But judge of their disappointment after being on the road twenty two or three days expecting for the last ten to come out on Carson River, their food all consumed, they came out on the Humboldt, and asking, "How far to the mines?" Our answer, "Between four and five hundred miles!"[46]

Byron McKinstry, *1849*

View of Hastings Cutoff after summer rain.

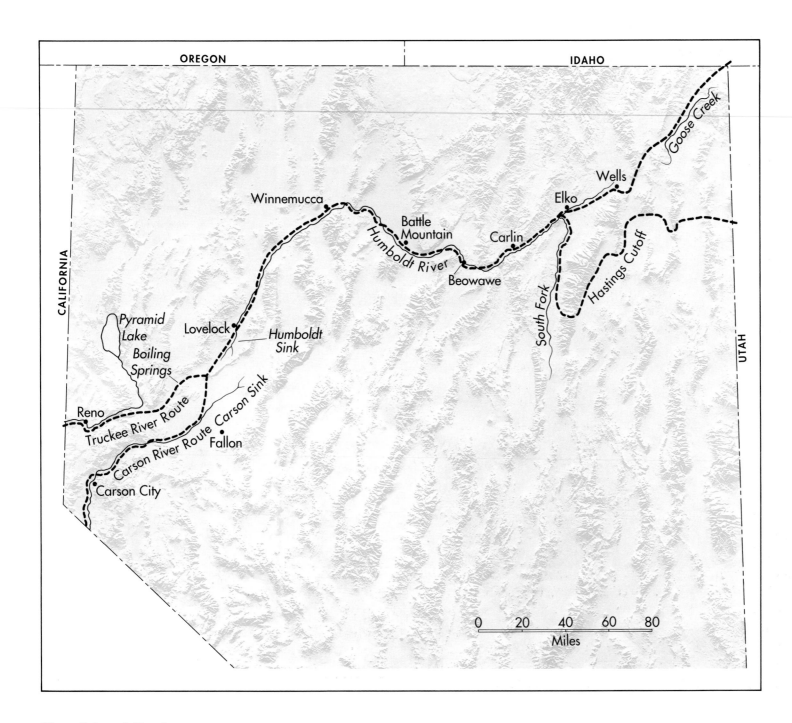

The trail through Nevada.

The main trail enters Nevada in the far northeast corner of the state. It then crosses over a series of major and minor mountain divides to join Goose Creek and Rock Creek, which lead to the Humboldt River near present-day Wells, Nevada. The crossing of Nevada was possible only because of the Humboldt, which headed on a near diagonal across the

T H E   N E V A D A   C R O S S I N G 5

state toward Sacramento. It is a miracle that a river could cross Nevada at all in an east-west direction, given the endless north-south system of mountain ranges it needed to penetrate.

The Humboldt River, or Mary's River, as it was originally named, and its route to California, was first discovered by a Virginia trapper, Joseph Walker, who used it to and from California in 1833 and 1834. Since he drew no map and since the route wasn't used again for ten years, it existed only in rumor to the first party of emigrants, the Bartleson-Bidwell party of 1841, who became thoroughly lost trying to find it. The connection of the Salt Lake Basin to this river crossed over several divides and confusing terrain. Walker himself found the route again when he returned as chief guide for the Joseph Chiles party in 1843.

The Humboldt River just barely served as a lifeline across Nevada. The soil along its banks was alkali and dusty to the extreme, yielding a very poor quality of grass. Unlike most rivers the emigrants were familiar with, which became larger as they went down-stream, the Humboldt maintained its skimpy width and volume to the end. There are few tributaries to feed it, and the heat and soft soil absorb or evaporate any contributions they might make. The result is a foul-tasting, long, thin pond with a stagnant current increasingly laden with minerals as one progresses across Nevada. The river seemed to have no fish, only frogs.

Since the Humboldt hardly supported the few Indian tribes along its banks, the presence of emigrant travel became a real threat. For the first time in the migration, a general state of hostility existed between Indian and emigrant. Compared to the Plains Indians, who had the mobility provided by horses, the Goshiutes, Paiutes, and Washoes lived on the river and barely eked out a living by hunting rabbits, catching frogs, and gathering what little vegetation they could find. The river was their lifeline, and the passing of emigrant trains threatened their existence by using up the precious resources, using the same campsites, and spoiling the water by careless livestock control. It is not difficult to imagine that the passage of 60,000 draft animals down the Humboldt in 1849 would completely destroy the ecosystem along the river. The Digger Indians didn't actually harm many emigrants as they didn't have fire-arms, just bows and arrows, but they waged war on the draft animals by shooting arrows into them at night. The Indians ate the wounded abandoned animals. The weakened condition of the remaining animals caused by the poor grass and alkaline water, not to mention the 1,700 miles already traveled, often forced emigrants to abandon wagon contents and, in some cases, the entire wagon.

At the western end of the map, a fork in the trail can be seen. This is the end of the Humboldt River. Here, its western progress is finally stopped by the Humboldt Mountain range and it backs up into a huge salty swamp and disappears into the Humboldt sink. The two routes across the waterless forty-mile desert to the next river systems, either the Truckee or Carson rivers, are shown leading to two separate routes to California.

The trail coming in from the far right side and taking a dip south around the Ruby Mountains is the Hastings cutoff. It has just crossed the Bonneville Salt Flats, a ninety-mile waterless playa. The detour around the Ruby Mountains could have been avoided if Hastings had not missed the short connection between his trail and the main trail near present-day Wells, Nevada, an easy day's march. It took an extra two weeks of hard travel to go around the mountains.

PLATE 48.

This deep gash, about fifty feet wide and over one mile long, shows how soft and light the soil is in this area. The original trail began by breaking the surface soil. Wind and a small amount of water runoff then eroded the trail into this seven-foot-deep trough. The fine dust in the soil of this area was an extreme hardship for both emigrants and animals. This trough is located in Thousand Springs Valley and is on the overland connection to join the Humboldt River at Wells, Nevada.

Deeply eroded ruts near Wells, Nevada.

PLATE 49.

My friend Studebaker says it took him more than five months to make the trip. I beat him, because it took me just 100 days from St. Jo. Missouri to Hangtown. The reason I beat him so much was because he drove horses and I came with a team of oxen, and engineered it my-self. Cattle always out-traveled horses on that long and trying journey.[47]

J. M. Stephen T. Gage, *1853*

John Mohler Studebaker would later return east and organize an automobile company.

On the trail, leaving Thousand Springs Valley, near Wells, Nevada.

PLATE 50.

The reader should not imagine the Humboldt to be a rapid mountain stream, with its cool and limpid waters rushing down the rocks of steep inclines, with here and there beautiful cascades and shady pools under mountain evergreens, where the sun never intrudes and where the speckled trout loves to sport. While the water of such a stream is fit for the gods, that of the Humboldt is not good for man nor beast. With the exception of a short distance from its source, it has the least perceptible current. There is not a fish nor any other living thing to be found in its waters, and there is not timber enough in three hundred miles of its desolate valley to make a snuff-box, or sufficient vegetation along its bank to shade a rabbit, while its waters contain the alkali to make soap for a nation, and, after winding its sluggish way through a desert within a desert, it sinks, diasappears, and leaves inquisitive man to ask how, why, when and where.[48]

Reuben Shaw, *1849*

Headwaters of the Humboldt River, Wells, Nevada.

PLATE 51.

Emigrants followed the Humboldt River for about 350
miles. Never much wider than in the photo, between
fifteen and twenty feet, its average depth was about
one foot. The route was cursed by all for its choking
dust, alkali water, and hostile Indians. The trail followed
both sides of the river for most of the Nevada crossing.
Since most of Nevada is unsuitable for farming, much
of the trail is still visible either as a ranch road or a two-
track, usually close to the main highway. Compared to
the trail in Wyoming, the dust is extremely fine and
irritating. Because it is about six inches deep in many
places it is not as popular among trail enthusiasts for
driving.

Humboldt River, 120 miles from source.

PLATE 52.

This part of the journey is considered very dangerous as the traveler is obliged to pass through the root digger tribe a nation of Indians cammence on the head waters of the Humboldt and is continued to the settlements of California. These Indians are wild and verry hostile, they lurk along the river for the purpos of stealing stock, many of them have bin killed by the mountaineers and are no more regarded by them than a woolf—they are generally small in stature ill formed and verry ugly features. Many of them are covered with hair so mutch so as to have the appearance of an orang-outang. Their feet is thick and of a bean or corn shape and almost as hard as a hoof. Their weapons are the bow and arrow sharp pointed stick and sharp flints. They open the graves of the dead that are buried in their land for the purpose of stealing the garments which are buried with them.[49]

Jay Green, *1852*

A man with his wife came into camp last night on foot, packing what little property they had left on a single ox, the sole remaining animal of their team; but I was informed of a worse case than this by some packers, who said they passed a man and his wife about 11 miles back who were on foot, toiling through the hot sand, the man carrying the blankets and other necessaries, and his wife carrying their only child in her arms, having lost all their team.[50]

Eleazer Stillman Ingalls, *1850*

Trail passing through KOA campground, near Elko, Nevada.

PLATE 53.

In the afternoon we moved our camp about five miles down the Humboldt. We now experienced some of the difficulties and dangers scarcely dreamed of in the early part of our journey. A virulent diarrhea prevails among the emigrants. Several of our company are quite sick, some of whom require constant care, making double work for those who attend the camp. The teams must have food as well as rest, and it is no small task to explore in advance for pasture. They must also be guarded with the utmost vigilance against Indians who, though seldom seen are constantly prowling around us. And those who are able to attend to this duty are almost entirely deprived of sleep. Our provisions too are nearly exhausted, each one having his daily ration, which is hardly sufficient to sustain life, much less satisfy hunger. The result is that the laughter, wit and song, which formerly cheered the camp, has given way to an unsocial, morose, and sometimes fault-finding spirit.[51]

John Steele, *August 21, 1849*

Probable trail site through Elko, Nevada.

PLATE 54.

In this view, the trail is most likely in the river bottom.
Carlin Canyon was created by a loop in the Humboldt
River less than one mile long. In spite of this, the river
had to be crossed seven times while in the canyon. The
Interstate 80 viaduct shown here avoided the canyon
by piercing a tunnel through the loop to open country
on the other side.

Humboldt River in Carlin Canyon, Nevada.

PLATE 55.

It is a matter of astonishment to me that cattle can live, far less work [with] apparently no grass; as our cattle have had for many weeks past. I am sure that if cattle were taken from good eating on pasture such as they have in the States and transferred to such as ours have had to live and work on for many weeks past, they would fast and starve before they could be induced to eat this.[52]

Joseph Middleton, *September 10, 1849*

Exit from Carlin, Nevada.

PLATE 56.

The grave of Lucinda Duncan was moved to the top of this small hill in 1906 when the Central Pacific railroad laid a new track over the old grave site. Based upon legend, and known as the Maiden's Grave, train conductors would tell stories to passengers about the nineteen-year-old girl, Lucinda Duncan, who lost her life in the journey to California. The large cross was erected in 1950 by the railroad so that passengers could more easily see the site. A contrary story however, disputes the legend.

Lucinda Duncan was my grandmother. I have known the story of her death all my life. I heard it from my mother, Melinda Duncan Thompson Robertson and from my half sisters. All who told it to me were on the wagon train with Lucinda coming west to California in the spring of 1863. I have told it several times to feature writers and it has been published once or twice. My story has never replaced the legend. Lucinda Duncan was not a girl of 17 or 18. She was a grandmother of 70 and she died near the Humboldt River with her children and grandchildren about her. . . .

There were 40 wagons that left Missouri that spring—all Duncans. . . . My grandmother, Lucinda Duncan, headed the wagons, she was the revered one and they gave her the place of honor. Then too, they knew ther would be less dust at the head of the train. . . .

I do not know the date my grandmother died but I do know what killed her. It was an aneurism of the heart.[53]

Iva Rader

Crescent Valley, Maidens Grave, and Union Pacific Railroad, near Beowawe, Nevada.

PLATE 57.

A very heart rendering scene has just taken place within 100 yards of our camp. A man came out from California to meet his wife who was crossing the plains with cattle &c., he arrived here at 3 o'clock this afternoon to find her dying of Bilious fever, although speechless she seemed to recognize him, looking at him for some considerable time, she put her arms around his neck and smiled, at 8 o'clock she died leaving three children she had brought with her, the eldest not yet four years old and she but 23, it was indeed a sad sight to see the poor husband in his anguish, he seems completely broken down, our women have gone over to their camp to assist in laying her out for burial far, far away from her home, a sister of the husband who was coming out with the wife had died some time since on the way.[54]

Henry Sheldon Anable, *August 28, 1852*

South Humboldt trail, Granite Point, near Battle Mountain, Nevada.

PLATE 58.

The Dust! no person can have the least idea, by a written description—it certainly is intolerable—but that does not half express my meaning—we eat it, drink it, breath it, night and day, the atmosphere being loaded with it. It effects people's eyes—but everybody had horribly sore lips—in fact, that is the greatest bane of the route.[55]

Dr. J. S. Shepherd, *1850*

It [dust] was nearly up to the hub of our wagons in many places and we are almost blinded by the dust from it. This dust is very bad on the eyes causing soreness and inflammation. . . . Never saw such dust! In some places it was actually to the top of the forewheels! Fine white dust, more like flour. Our men were a perfect fright, being literally covered with it. Our poor animals staggered along through the blinding dust, coughing at every step! . . . It is very cold in the mountains, a fresh breeze is blowing all of the time, and the dust . . . how can I give any idea of it? We are almost blinded by it. My eyes are very sore. We all have to wear veils or goggles, some wear handkerchiefs over their faces and with all we are almost choked and blinded. It tries my patience more than anything else![56]

Anonymous Diary, *1850*

Dust protection at Hawes Stage Station ruins, Nevada.

PLATE 59.

The Pioneer Line was an ambitious commercial plan to provide quick and luxurious passage to California. It was basically ill-conceived. The elaborate stage coaches boasting elliptical springs were too heavy, the supplies needed greatly underestimated, and the captains too inexperienced. The first train, consisting of twenty carriages and twenty-two baggage and supply wagons left Independence in late April 1849, bound for California. The estimated time of travel was fifty-five to sixty days (compared to five months by conventional wagon train). Mules were used because they were supposed to be faster. The heavy wagons immediately got bogged down in the muddy road along the Platte as the mules couldn't handle the weight of the passengers, and they ended up walking. Eventually the train disbanded, the remaining supplies divided, and the passengers left to walk the remaining distance to California.

At night, a man came to our camp who had taken a passage at St. Louis in the Pioneer line of spring wagons, which were advertised to go through in sixty days. He was on foot, armed with a knife and pistol, and carried in a small knapsack all this wordly goods, except a pair of blankets, which were rolled up on his shoulders. He told us that at Willow Springs their mules gave out, and there was a general distribution of property, a small proportion of the passengers only obtaining mules, the rest being obliged to go a thousand miles without supplies, in the best manner they could, trusting to luck and the emigrants for provisions. The passengers had each paid two hundred dollars for their passage, but now, like the Irishman on the tow-path, were obliged to work it out. No emigrant would see him suffer under such circumstances, and we cheerfully shared our poor fare with him. [57]

Alonzo Delano, *July 27, 1849*

Ruts intersecting embankment of U.S. Route 40, Lovelock, Nevada.

PLATE 60.

The Humboldt River stops flowing at the Humboldt Sink near Lovelock, Nevada. Here it backs up into a huge salt marsh caused by a natural dike and sinks into the ground. The swamplands created meadows of grass and drinkable water used in preparation for the desert crossing to come. It was an active staging area with teams continuously entering and leaving. After filling wagons with cut grass and barrels of water, the forty-mile desert crossing usually began late in the afternoon so that as much as possible of the twenty-four-hour trek could be accomplished during the cooler night hours. Emigrants reached this section of trail in late August when afternoon temperatures could reach 100 degrees.

. . . On arriving at the Sink of the Humboldt, a great disappointment awaited us. We had known nothing of the nature of that great wonder except what we had been told by those who knew no more about it than ourselfs. In place of a great rent in the earth, into which the waters of the river plunged with a terrible roar (as pictured in our imagination), there was found a mud lake ten miles long and four or five miles wide, a veritable sea of slime, a "slough of despond," an ocean of ooze, a bottomless bed of alkali poison, which emited a nauseous odor and presented the appearance of utter desolation. The croaking of frogs would have been a redeeming feature of the place, but no living thing disturbed the silence and solitude of the lonely region. There were mysteries and wonders hovering over and around the Sink of the Humboldt, but there was neither beauty nor grandeur in connection with it, for a more dreary or desolate spot could not be found on the face of the earth.[58]

Reuben Shaw, *1849*

Humboldt Sink and Mountain Range, terminus of the Humboldt River, Pershing County, Nevada.

PLATE 61.

There are two routes through this desert: one to the Carson River and the other to the Truckee. Emigrants could follow either river to the Sierra Mountains in California. The distance was not impossible as they were used to 15–20–mile days. However, the extreme heat, sections of soft sand, lack of forage, and, most important, the weakened state of the animals caused by poor grass and water while traveling down the Humboldt, made this crossing especially dangerous.

The destruction of property upon this part of the road is beyond all computation. Abandoned wagons literally crowded the way for twenty miles, and the dead animals are so numerous, that I have counted 50 carcasses within a distance of 40 rods. The desert from side to side is strewn with goods of every name. The following articles however, are peculiarly abundant; log chains, wagons, wagon irons, iron bound water casks, cooking implements, all kinds of dishes and hollow ware, cooking stoves and utensils, boots and shoes, clothing of all kinds, even life preservers, trunks and boxes, tin bakers, books, guns, pistols, gunlocks, gun barrels. Edged tools, planes, augers, and chisels, mill and cross cut saws, good geese feathers in heaps, or blowing over the desert, feather beds, canvas tents and wagon covers.[59]

Franklin Langworthy, *1850*

Entrance to Forty-Mile Desert, Truckee River route.

PLATE 62.

As it takes 24 hours to cross the desert, it was thought best to start in the evening, so we left camp an hour before sun down.[60]

Helen McCowen Carpenter, *1856*

Jornadas

In some localities 50 or 60 miles, and even greater distances, are frequently traversed without water; these long stretches are called by the Mexicans "Journadas" or day's journey. There is one in New Mexico called "Journada del Muerto," which is 78½ miles in length, where in a dry season, there is not a drop of water; yet with the proper care, this drive can be made with ox or mule teams, and without loss or injury to the animals.

On arriving at the last camping-ground before entering upon the journada, all the animals should be as well rested and refreshed as possible. To insure this, they must be turned out upon the best grass that can be found, and allowed to eat and drink as much as they desire during the entire halt. Should the weather be very warm, and the teams composed of oxen, the march should not be resumed until it begins to cool in the afternoon. They should be carefully watered just previous to being hitched up and started out upon the journada, the water-kegs having been previously filled. The drive is then commenced, and continued during the entire night, with 10 or 15 minutes rest every two hours. About daylight a halt

should be made, and the animals immediately turned out to graze for two hours, during which time, especially if there is dew upon the grass, they will have become considerably refreshed, and may be put to the wagon again and driving until the heat becomes oppressive toward noon, when they are again turned out upon a spot where the grass is good, and, if possible where there are shade trees. About four o'clock P.M. they are again started, and the march continued into the night, as long as they can be driven without suffering. If, however, there should be dew, which is seldom the case on the plains, it would be well to turn out the animals several times during the second night, and by morning, if they are in good condition, the journada of 70 or 80 miles will have been passed without any great amount of suffering.[61]

from The Prairie Traveler: A Handbook for Overland Expeditions, *1859*

I had with me a pair of long top leather boots; these I filled with hay just as full as I could stuff them. . . . At 2 P.M., all being in readiness we saddled up and adjusting my boots, filled with hay, across my saddle, one boot on each side, I rode my horse out into the slough of water and with my tin cup filled each boot full of water.[62]

Lemuel C. McKeeby, *1850*

Night crossing, Forty-Mile Desert, Nevada.

PLATE 63.

The depression and the rock pile dam are the location of Boiling Springs, a very hot water source of alkaline water located at the midpoint of the forty-mile Truckee River route desert. The trail continues west through the low spot in the distant hills. An onion dehydration factory and a geothermal electric power plant now lease the property and are located about one hundred yards away. The water here, although disagreeable, could be used by animals and humans.

. . . at about 15 miles or half way from Waushee [Truckee] river to the first water near Marys Lake still exist a cauldron of Boiling water no steam issues from it [at] present but it stands in several pools boiling and again disappearing some of these pools have beautiful clear water Boiling in them and others emit Quantities of mud into one of these muddy pools my little water spaniel went poor fellow not Knowing that it was Boiling hot he deliberately walked in to the caldron to slake his thirst and cool his limbs when to his sad disappointment and my sorrow he scalded himself allmost instantly to death I felt more for his loss than any other animal I ever lost in my life as he had been my constant companion in all my wanderings since I Left Milwawkee and I vainly hoped to see him return to his old master in his native village (but such is the nature of all earthly hopes)[63]

James Clyman, *1844*

We visited the boiling springs, which are, indeed a great curiosity, with their waters foaming and gurgling, the noise of which at times, they tell me, may be heard at a half mile's distance. In one of them we saw the bones of a man who, being deranged, threw himself into it a year or two since, and immediately perished. A women and a child were also killed by falling into it last summer.[64]

Harriet S. Ward, *1853*

Boiling Springs ruins, Churchill County, Nevada.

PLATE 64.

The small pile of rocks in the lower left side is an un-marked grave. It is oriented in an east-west direction, as was the custom of the time. Usually the head of the deceased was toward the setting sun. Friends or rela-tives had to walk a considerable distance to obtain these rocks as there are none in the immediate area, which is deep sand. The scraps of iron are barrel hoops. Water barrels were abandoned when empty be-cause once the Truckee River was reached there would be ample water all the way to California. Interstate 80 traffic is in the background. In this last third of the journey, those who did not bring Vitamin C supple-ments such as vinegar or vegetables were apt to suffer from scurvy, as they were now 5 months on the trail. Pack trains, composed of single men on horseback and mule, were more likely to abandon sick members of their parties along the trail hoping that they would be aided by upcoming trains. The lack of family connec-tion and no wagons in which to carry the sick were probably the reasons for this questionable action.

The amount of suffering on the latter part of the route was almost incalculable. No one except those who saw or experienced it, can have any idea of its extent—sights, the thoughts of which, would make the blood chill in any human breast. After I left the train, I saw men sit-ting or lying by the roadside, sick with fevers or crip-pled by scurvy, begging of the passerby to lend them some assistance, but no one could do it. The winter was so near, that it was sure death literally, and the teams were all giving out, so that the thought of hauling them in the wagons was absurd. Nothing could be done, conse-quently they were left to a slow lingering death in the wilderness.[65]

James D. Lyon, *1849*

Unmarked emigrant grave and barrel hoops, near Wadsworth, Nevada.

PLATE 65.

The road now went in a more westerly direction, whereas in the last three or four days we had been traveling almost due south. At first we drove through low country, but gradually we climbed considerably higher. . . . The rocks had a peculiar formation, such as I had never saw before or since.[66]

Heinrich Lienhard, *1846*

Peculiar rocks, Forty-Mile Desert, Truckee River route.

PLATE 66.

. . . Took 2 hours rest about midnight and arrived to our great joy at the Salmon Trout [Truckee] River at 7 A.M. on Sunday Sept. 9, and once more had a refreshing draught of pure water and was gladdened by the sight of large majestic trees. The Salmon Trout being lined with the finest Cotton woods I ever saw. No one can imagine how delightful the sight of a tree is after such long stretches of desert, until they have tried it. We have seen very few of any kind since leaving the Platte, and what a luxury after our mules were taken care of, to lay down in their shade and make up our two nights loss of sleep, and hear the wind rustling their leaves and whistling among their branches.[67]

Elisha D. Perkins, *1849*

Cottonwood trees on Truckee River, end of Forty-Mile Desert.

PLATE 67.   *Oxen remains, Forty-Mile Desert, Carson River route.*

The dark humps of earth shown here are actually the remains of dead cattle or draft animals from the migration period. Small sections of decayed vertebrae still protrude from the soil; however, very little large bone material remains. This section of trail is about fifteen miles into the crossing.

PLATE 68. *Rocks placed at Salt Creek Crossing, Forty-Mile Desert, Carson River route.*

It is theorized that these rocks were placed by emigrants to stand on in order to help turn the wagon wheels by hand. The river bank here is very soft, and the wheels would sink deep into it. Salt Creek is midway in the Carson forty-mile desert route, and the thirsty animals had to forcibly be kept from drinking the water as it was poisonous.

PLATE 69.

These ruts are in the heart of the Carson Desert Route, where wagons spread out to avoid the dust. The fate of this section of trail is currently the subject of a dispute over whether or not the federal Bureau of Land Management should allow a Utah corporation to flood the area with water and create a salt evaporation pond.

Imagine to yourself a vast plain of sand and clay; the moon riding over you in silent grandeur, just renders visible by her light the distant mountains; the stinted sage, the salt lakes, cheating the thirsty traveler into the belief that water is near; yes, water it is, but poison to the living thing that stops to drink. . . . Burning wagons render still more hideous the solemn march; dead horses line the road, and living ones may be constantly seen, lapping and rolling the empty water casks (which have been cast away) for a drop of water to quench their burning thirst, or standing with drooping heads, waiting for death to relieve them of their tortures, or lying on the sand half buried, unable to rise, yet still trying. The sand hills are reached; then comes a scene of confusion and dismay. Animal after animal drops down. Wagon after wagon is stopped, the strongest animals taken out of the harness; the most important effects are taken out of the wagon and placed on their backs and all hurry away, leaving behind wagons, property and animals that, too weak to travel, lie and broil in the sun in agony of thirst until death relieves them. The owners hurry on with but one object in view, that of reaching the Carson River before the boiling sun shall reduce them to the same condition. Morning comes, and the light of day presents a scene more horrid than the rout of a defeated army; dead stock line the roads, wagons, rifles, tents, clothes, everything but food may be found scattered along the road; here an ox who standing famished against a wagon bed until nature could do no more, settles back into it and dies; and there a horse kicking out its last gasp in the burning sand, men scattered along the plain and stretched out among the dead stock like corpses, fill out the picture. The desert! You must see it and feel it on an August day, when legions have crossed it before you, to realize it in all its horrors. But heaven save you from the experience.

J. Ingalls, *1850*
[Inscription on a monument in the middle of Carson Forty-mile Desert]

Multiple tracks across Parren Flat, Carson Desert route.

PLATE 70.

Burning wagons, seen at a distance at night, were reported in emigrant diaries. It is not clear why they took precious time to destroy abandoned property. There was so much useful iron left on this desert that for many years junk dealers from the pioneer settlement of Reno would salvage the materials for resale. Wagon parts and tools were considerably prized. Most of the losses occurred at the twenty-mile mark where deep sand filled the route. This area is still peppered with rusted bits of iron.

The migration of 1850 encountered particularly huge losses on this section of trail. One diarist reported that he actually counted among dead animals 4,960 horses, 3,750 oxen, and 1,601 mules. In that same year, John Wood reported that all who traveled the Carson route estimated 3,000 abandoned wagons that season, three out of every four that entered the desert.[68]

The reasons for these great losses are several: the migration of 1849 involved 27,000 emigrants and 60,000 animals. Food was not a problem for either. Most emigrants overpacked; wagons were overloaded and provisions had to be jettisoned along the way. Because it was the wettest and coolest summer in remembered history, the animals found abundant grass along the Humboldt. The following year, 1850, the emigrants reacted to stories of overpacking by taking too little. Many ran out of supplies as early as Fort Laramie. In addition, the 45,000 emigrants and 100,000 animals traveling that year endured an exceedingly hot summer in western Nevada, so there was little grass. The Humboldt River's slim resources were so taxed by this traffic that both animals and emigrants arrived here undernourished and exhausted. Entrepreneurs would ride out to sell supplies to the thousands of travelers on foot, usually water, at outrageous prices, one account being fifteen dollars a glass.

Remains of burned wagon, Carson River route.

PLATE 71.

On the morning the company left its camp, near the border of the desert, a married lady came in on horseback, bringing several canteens for water. She had left her husband and only child late the evening before, some fifteen miles back suffering for water, and in her anxiety to hasten to the river, had lost the trail and traveled the whole night;—but with that love which a mother only commands for a helpless and suffering, aye, dying child, she refused assistance, and would not weary until the whole mission was fulfilled. She delayed but a moment until the vessels were filled, when being provided with a fresh horse, she flew with the speed of the arrow back to her suffering companion and dying child. This was an instance of personal devotion, and female heroism, I had never seen equalled.[69]

Richard Oglesby, *1849*

Campers on the trail, Forty-Mile Desert, Carson River route, deep sand section.

PLATE 72.

Soda Lake is located at the end of the Carson Desert route near where it joins the Carson River. The lake is situated inside an extinct volcanic crater with steep loose cinder walls, which make it almost impossible to walk down to the surface. The walls are about 200 feet high except for one spot near the drinkable water springs at the north base and trail.

We turned to the left from the road, passed over a ridge and there found a fresh water spring, also a salt water lake of about five miles in surcumpherance. This lake had a verry high rim or Ridge around it and had neither inlet or outlet and water is exceeding Salty.[70]

William H. Kilgore, *1850*

I wish California had sunk into the ocean before I had ever heard of it. Here I am alone, having crossed the desert, it is true, and got to some good water, but have nothing to eat all day, my companions scattered, our wagons left behind. That desert has played hell with us.[71]

James Wilkins, *1849*

Dead cat and barrel, Soda Lake, Churchill County, Nevada.

PLATE 73.   *On the trail, looking west, Dayton, Nevada.*

In Dayton the trail goes straight through Main Street and is the dusty road seen climbing the hill in the background.
An official Nevada historical marker can be seen at the end of this street.

PLATE 74.   *Truckee River route approaching Reno sewer plant, Nevada.*

In this view the trail is going through the sewer plant. High-rise gambling casinos are in the background. Jameson's Station, an emigrant trading post, was located where the road enters the plant. It was built in 1852 and was the first permanent settlement in Reno. During emigrant times the large valley Reno is located in was called Truckee Meadows and was a huge swamp. This is the mouth of the Truckee River canyon which the trail has been following for thirty miles.

PLATE 75.

The photograph is taken from Rattlesnake Mountain
on what used to be Short Ranch. This former campsite,
located in the center of the picture, was a resting spot
with good grass and water. The Donner Party camped
here just before it ascended the Sierra into the Truckee,
California, area where half its members perished in the
winter of 1846–47. The housing development that covers this site today is called Donner Spring.

Donner Springs campsite, Reno, Nevada.

PLATE 76

The Carson River route follows along the base of the Sierra Nevada Mountains in this view and will turn right up into the valleys following the river to the summit. The route was opened by a Mormon battalion recruited by the government to assist in the anticipated war with Mexico. They had marched from Santa Fe to California in 1846, but since there was no real war, they saw no action and spent the winter in California waiting for spring and their return to Salt Lake City (barely established). In 1848 they headed east and after having three scouts murdered by Indians, discovered a new pass over the Sierra that would connect to the headwaters of the Carson River. On the east side of the mountains they followed the river to the Carson Sink, in the same vicinity as the Humboldt Sink, and an easy connection to the Humboldt River, which they followed east (backward) to the Salt Lake City area. The Carson route would prove more popular to the majority of traffic which was headed for the southern gold fields as it crossed the Sierra in a more favorable proximity.

Moving forward, we passed a remarkable hot spring. It gushes from the base of a mountain, between strata of horizontal rocks, in nearly a continuous thin sheet; the water being near the boiling point, and the stream nearly a mile in breadth. . . .

Moved along up the valley. It is an oasis of great extent, green, romantic, and beautiful, situated in the midst of vast deserts and barren mountains. The Carson river runs a serpentine course through the valley the banks being everywhere fringed with a luxuriant growth of willows. The valley lies north and south, is of an oval form, and is covered with a natural growth of excellent grass. On the west side, the mountain rises to a great height, and from its base spring a great number of small creeks of pure and exceedingly cold water. These rills, running swiftly over pebbled beds, cross the road at short intervals, and meandering through the grassy plain, fall at length into the Carson river.

At ten in the morning, we met a train of sixty Mormons, with four hundred horses and mules, on their way to Salt Lake. These Mormons informed us, that two days previously they had killed and scalped six Digger Indians, in revenge for thirty mules which the Indians had stolen from them. They took from the Diggers five horses, though they were not the same as those they lost, and did not know whether the Indians they had killed were those concerned in the theft, or otherwise. This was executing justice upon the same principle as practiced by the Indians. When an Indian is killed by a white man, the tribe to which he belonged never feel satisfied until the life of some white man atones for the offence. In this case, any other individual answers their purpose precisely as well as the identical murderer.[72]

Franklin Langworthy, *1850*

On the trail, Walleys Hot Springs, Genoa, Nevada.

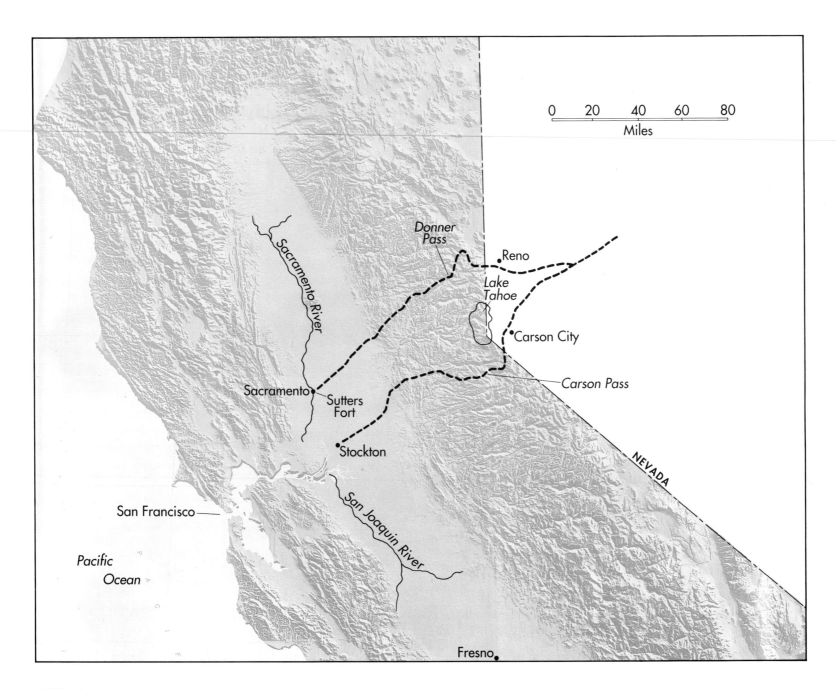

Donner Pass

Reno

Lake Tahoe

Carson City

Carson Pass

Sacramento River

Sacramento

Sutters Fort

Stockton

San Joaquin River

San Francisco

Pacific Ocean

Fresno

NEVADA

0   20   40   60   80
Miles

California

If travel went according to schedule, at an average of fifteen miles per day, emigrants would reach the California border around late August. There is no easy way to enter northern California. Being fifty miles across, 400 miles long, and at right angles to the direction of travel, the Sierra Mountains effectively block the entrance. All passes from

C A L I F O R N I A

the east have steep ascents, are snow-clogged in winter, and are over 7,000 feet in elevation. Until wagons could be taken into California, however, an official trail could not be claimed to exist. The Bartleson-Bidwell party of 1841 and the Chiles-Walker party of 1843 both failed in their attempts and had to abandon the wagons. Over two travel seasons, the Stevens party of 1844–45 succeeded in crossing the Sierras with wagons, even though it required disassembling them and hauling them over in pieces.

The emigrants eventually found passes by following the Truckee and Carson rivers to their sources. The Carson, Donner, Coldstream Canyon, and Roller (so-called because a log pulley was used at the summit to drag the wagons over the top) passes were all used, depending upon whether one wanted to go to the southern or northern goldfields, or Sacramento.

Once over the passes, the long downhill run to the Central Valley or goldfields proved almost as difficult as the ascent. Since the western slopes of the Sierra get most of the rain, many river systems were created which in turn created deep valleys and high ridges. These were not always in the desired direction of travel, thus causing more difficult vertical ascents over divides. Furthermore, in order to stay out of river bottoms, the trail followed along rough, angled, granite surfaces, which paralleled the Yuba and American rivers. It is eighty miles from the Nevada border to Sacramento, most all of it densely forested mountain downslope.

PLATE 77.

On the front side of the tree are several hand-made signs, dating back to the 1920s identifying this tree as the Donner campsite. They were placed over the years by both amateur and professional historians. It was at this site that George and Jacob Donner and their wives perished in 1845. The rest of the Donner-Reed Party was trapped at present-day Donner Lake, about ten miles away, where ironically there is a park, lake, and pass named after the Donners. Other families in the train, the Murphys, Reeds, and Breems, survived eight months trapped in record snow depths before rescue parties from Sacramento could reach them. The survivors resorted to cannibalism in order to stay alive. In 1990, the Universisty of Nevada, Reno, made extensive archeological studies around this tree. No hard evidence was found to substantiate that this was indeed the correct location of the campsite.

Thursday 31 last of the year, may we with God's help spend the comeing year better than the past which we purpose to do if Almighty God will deliver us from our present dredful situation. . . . morning fair, now cloudy . . . looks like another snow storm.

Jany. 1st 1847 . . . Commenced snowing last night . . . sun peeps out at times provisions geting scant dug up a hide from under the snow yesterday for Milt.

Frid. [January] 26th . . . plenty hides but the folks will not eat them we eat with them with a tolerable good appetite. Thanks be to Almighty God. Amen. Mrs Murphy said here yesterday that [she] thought she would commence on Milt and eat him. I dont [think] that she has done so yet, it is distressing the Donnos told the California folks that they [would] commence to eat the dead people 4 days ago, if they did not succeed that day or next in finding their cattle then under ten or twelve feet of snow and did not know the spot or near it. I suppose they have done so ere this time.[73]

Patrick Breen, *1846*

Tree where Joseph Donner pitched his tent and perished, Alder Creek, California.

PLATE 78.   *Exit point from Prosser Creek Reservoir, California*

Prior to the reservoir, the trail followed Prosser Creek through this section between Reno and Truckee, California. The most direct route would have been to follow the Truckee River all the way to the Sierra Summit, but the canyon walls were too steep, thus forcing travel into the river bottom. The Stevens party of 1844 did travel the river bottom and had to cross the Truckee twenty-seven times in this section. Travel in rivers was to be avoided in that it was always rough and rocky, the water ice cold, and the oxen would suffer hoof rot.

PLATE 79.   *On the trail, Donner Lake, approching Sierra Nevada range.*

The granite wall of the Sierra Mountains may be seen in the background, and the low spot under the sign is Donner Pass. Although the pass is only 7,000 feet in altitude, not much higher than South Pass in Wyoming, the steep approach was unprecedented. At times the slope was 45 degrees. Alternative passes were eventually used to the left of the high peak. The distance from this spot on Donner Lake to the summit is only two miles, but it would require two days of travel inching up the slope.

PLATE 80.

The first wagons to enter California would pass up the gully and underneath the present rock wall, which was built in 1866 to support the Central Pacific Railroad tracks. It is known as China Wall as it was built primarily by Chinese labor. It is located at the summit of the range. The Stevens party of 1844 who numbered about fifty members, were the first to use this route and this pass. They were told of the existence of a river by an Indian called Truckee whom they met back at the Humboldt Sink. He suggested a route across the Forty-mile desert and up the river (which would be named after him) to this point.

On the steep uphill approach to this pass a ten-foot vertical granite wall had to be surmounted. It is still not clear how the wagons were taken over this obstacle, but it seems likely they were unpacked and partially dismantled. Their efforts can be more fully appreciated given the presence of two feet of snow in the mountains on a very late November 24th crossing.

The Stevens party were not able to get all the wagons across the summit before winter snows began; they abandoned half of them along with one member, back downhill at Donner Lake. Young Mose Shallenberger spent the winter alone, guarding the wagons and surviving on his wits. The pass should properly be named after Stevens since the Donner brothers died before reaching this point, as well as to being years later in time, 1846.

This pass was abandoned two years later for a higher, yet less steep summit along this same ridge, about two miles away.

A fiber optics cable was laid up this slope and the large boulders in this view were placed on top of it and the trail.

A long time to go about two miles over our rough, new-made road . . . over the rough rocks, in some places, and so smooth in others, that the oxen would slip and fall on their knees; the blood from their feet and knees staining the rocks they passed over. Mother and I walked, (we were so sorry for the poor, faithful oxen) all those two miles—all our clothing being packed on the horses' backs. It was a trying time—the men swearing at their teams, and beating them most cruelly, all along that rugged way.[74]

Sarah Ide, *1845*

Boulders on the trail, Donner Pass summit, California.

PLATE 81.

The downslope of the Sierra Nevada into the Central
Valley of California and the goldfields is typified by the
terrain in this view. An uneven rocky surface with random boulders, endless drop-off ledges, and thickets of
dense trees caused slow travel as one ridge after another was traversed. Trail ruts are not visible on the
hard granite surfaces. Consequently, the route is located by following rust stains in the rock caused by
small flecks of iron from the wagon wheel rims. The
trail came down the existing road and turned left
through the parked cars. In the grove of trees on the
left is further trail evidence in the form of notches of
bark removed from tree trunks as wagon wheel hubs
came too close.

Roller-blade skater on the trail, Big Bend Station, Yuba River, California.

PLATE 82.

Emigrant Gap is located at the curve in the railroad track where the trail would cross the tracks and plunge down the mountain into the Bear Valley seen at the far right. The descent required everything from dragging the plentiful trees as brakes, to tying ropes on the wagons, and snubbing onto tree trunks allowing the wagons to inch downhill as rope was slackened. The gap is located at a low spot along the ridge seen here, where today the Southern Pacific Railroad and Interstate 80 are squeezed into close proximity as they straddle the narrow ridge separating the valleys of Bear and American rivers, on the timbered downslope of the Sierra.

The California goldfields are within five miles of this view, and many roads split off the main trail leading to the creeks and river bottoms of the Placer mines. Women also took these jumping off opportunities into the gold diggings rather than continue on to the more civilized central valley with the intent of somehow getting their share of the large quantities of gold being removed from the river bottoms.

A smart woman can do very well in this country—true there are not many comforts and one must work all the time and work hard but [there] is plenty to do and good pay. If I was in Boston now and know what I now know of California I would come out here if I had to hire the money to bring me out. It is the only country I ever was in where a woman received anything like a just compensation for work. . . .

I have made about $18,000 worth of pies—about one-third of this has been clear profit. One year I dragged my own wood off the mountain and chopped it, and I have never had so much as a child to take a step for me in this country. $11,000 I baked in one little iron skillet, a considerable portion by a campfire, without the shelter of a tree from the broiling sun.[75]

from California Emigrant Letters,
Letter to Cathrine Oliver, *1850*

Emigrant Gap, Placer County, California.

PLATE 83.

John Sutter, a Swiss emigrant, began building his fort in 1841 after receiving a 47,000-acre land grant from the governor of California, Juan Alvarado. California was controlled by Mexico at this time, and the Central Valley, where Sacramento would soon be created, was too far inland to be effectively managed by the government. Sutter promised to settle the land and develop commerce for Mexico. The original fort was 320 feet long and 150 wide with adobe wall 18 feet high. It was larger than any of the forts along the trail. The fort served as the hub for agriculture, shipping, tanning, lumber and fishing industries developed by Sutter. His empire grew to 150,000 acres after a second governor added to the first land grant. Emigrants on the Overland Trail were welcomed to the fort for rest, provisions, and orientation to California, as Sutter hoped they would settle in his territory and contribute to his economic empire.

It was Sutter who organized and funded the six separate rescue teams who returned to the snow-filled Sierra Mountains to locate the stranded Donner-Reed party and bring back the forty-seven survivors.

In 1846, California became independent of Mexico, with the Bear Flag revolt. Sutter, seen as a Mexican sympathizer, lost control of his fort. His economic collapse ironically was completed when gold was discovered at one of his sawmills in the foothills of the Sierra. The flood of gold miners stole his livestock, raided his fields, and squatted on his land. He was paid $7,000 for the fort, a fraction of its value, and the original Mexican land grant declared invalid. His land would eventually become part of the new homestead giveaway program.

"Come along, come along—don't be alarmed,
Uncle Sam is rich enough to give us all a farm."

From a popular emigrant camp song

St. Francis Elementary School jog-a-thon, Sutters Fort, Sacramento, California.

We reached Sacramento on November 4, 1849, just six months and ten days after leaving Clinton, Iowa. . . . . Upon the whole I enjoyed the trip, in spite of its hardships and dangers and the fear and dread that hung as a pall over us every hour. Although not so thrilling as were the experiences of many who suffered in reality what we feared, but escaped, I like every other pioneer, love to live over again, in memory those romantic months, an revisit, in fancy, the scenes of the journey.[76]

Catherine Haun, 1849

1. Greg MacGregor, "Traces of the Pioneers: Photographing the Overland Trail," *California History* [California Historical Society, San Francisco] (Winter 1991-92): 343.

2. Quoted in Sandra L. Myres, "I Too Have Seen the Elephant: Women on the Overland Trails," *Overland Journal* 4, no. 4 [Oregon-California Trails Association, Independence, Mo.] (1986): 26.

3. MacGregor, "Traces of the Pioneers," p. 339.

4. George Stewart, *The California Trail* (Lincoln: University of Nebraska, 1962), p. 309.

5. Quoted in Jo Ann Levy, "We Were Forty-Niners Too: Women in the California Gold Rush," *Overland Journal* 6, no. 3 (1988): 29.

6. Quoted in Thomas Hunt, *Ghost Trails to California* (Las Vegas, Nev.: Las Vegas Publications, 1974), p. 65.

7. Ibid., p. 31.

8. Randolf B. Marcy, *The Prairie Traveler: A Handbook for Overland Expeditions* (New York: Harper & Brothers, 1859), p. 12.

9. Myres, "I Too Have Seen the Elephant," p. 32.

10. J. S. Holliday, ed. *The World Rushed In* (New York: Touchstone Books, 1981), p. 95.

11. Marcy, *The Prairie Traveler,* p. 45.

12. Ibid., p. 45.

13. Merrill J. Mattes, *The Great Platte River Road* (Lincoln: University of Nebraska, 1969), p. 268.

14. Lillian Schlissel, *Women's Diaries of the Westward Journey* (New York: Schocken Books, 1992), p. 207.

15. Quoted in Richard and Mary Ann Gehling, "Platte River Itinerary, 1860," *Overland Journal* 5, no. 3 (1985): 4.

16. Invard Henry Eide, *Oregon Trail* (Chicago: Rand McNally, 1972).

17. Martin, "The Lighter Side of Trail Experience," p. 11.

18. Holliday, *The World Rushed In,* p. 164.

19. Quoted in Dorothy Dustin, "Narcissa Whiteman and Friends: New York to Fort Wiliams 1836," *Overland Journal* 8, no. 1 (1990): 24.

20. Marcy, *The Prairie Traveler,* p. 8.

21. Francis Parkman, *The Oregon Trail* (New York: George Putnam, 1849).

22. Myres, "I Too Have Seen the Elephant," p. 30.

23. Aubrey Haines, *Historic Sites Along the Oregon Trail* (Saint Louis: Patrice Press, 1981) p. 169.

24. Quoted in Peter D. Olch, "Treading the Elephant's Tail, Medical Problems on the Overland Trails," *Overland Journal* 6, no. 1 (1988): 26.

25. Schlissel, *Women's Diaries,* p. 182.

26. Marcy, *The Prairie Traveler,* p. 17.

27. Schlissel, *Women's Diaries,* p. 84.

28. Haines, *Historic Sites,* p. 198.

29. Quoted in Richard and Mary Gehling, "Wind Wagons West," *Overland Journal* 11, no. 4 (1993): 6.

30. Munkers, "Devil's Gate," p. 4.

31. Quoted in Mike Brown and Beverly Gorney, eds., *Headed West* (Salt Lake City: Sweetwater County Travel and Tourism Board, 1992), p. 61.

32. *Overland Journal* 8, no. 4 (1990): 34.

33. Holliday, *The World Rushed In,* p. 209.

34. John MacFaragher, *Women and Men on the Overland Trail* (New Haven: Yale University Press, 1979), p. 175.

35. Quoted in Robert Munkers, "Fort Bridger," *Overland Journal* 8, no. 2, 1990, p. 26.

36. Ibid., p. 33.

37. Ibid., p. 31.

38. Olch, "Treading the Elephant's Tail," p. 26.

39. Quoted in Charles W. Martin, Sr., "Diary of Enoch Conyers 1852," *Overland Journal* 5, no. 3 (1987): 9.

40. Quoted in Devere and Helen Helfrich, and Thomas Hunt, *Emigrant Trails West* (Reno: Trails West, 1984), p. 59.

41. Schlissel, *Women's Diaries,* p. 189.

42. Helfrich and Hunt, *Emigrant Trails West,* p. 60.

43. Schlissel, *Women's Diaries,* p. 226.

44. Helfrich and Hunt, *Emigrant Trails,* p. 64.

45. Ibid., p. 92.

46. Ibid., p. 90.

47. Quoted in Fred K. Fox, "John Mohler Studebaker's 1853 Overland Journey from Indiana to California," *Overland Journal* 8, no. 4 (1990): 35.

48. Hunt, *Ghost Trails to California,* p. 108.

49. Hunt, *Ghost Trails to California,* p. 50.

50. Quoted in Harold Curran, *Fearful Crossing* (Las Vegas: Nevada Publications, 1982), p. 130.

51. Helfrich and Hunt, *Emigrant Trails West,* p. 96.

52. Ibid., p. 45.

53. Curran, *Fearful Crossing,* p. 93.

54. Quoted in Don Buck, "Diary Excerpt," *Overland Journal* 6, no. 1 (1988): 33.

55. Curran, *Fearful Crossing,* p. 45.

56. Olch, "Treading the Elephant's Tail," p. 28.

57. Helfrich and Hunt, *Emigrant Trails West,* p. 74.

58. Reuben Shaw, *Across the Plains in Forty Nine,* edited by Milton Quaife (Chicago: R. R. Donnelley & Sons, 1948).

59. Curran, *Fearful Crossing,* p. 181.

60. Ibid., p. 143.

61. Marcy, *The Prairie Traveler,* p. 29.

62. Ibid., p. 139

63. Hunt, *Ghost Trails to California,* p. 183.

64. Curran, *Fearful Crossing,* p. 148.

65. Olch, "Treading the Elephant's Tail," p. 27.

66. Curran, *Fearful Crossing,* p. 145.

67. Ibid., p. 152.

68. Stewart, *The California Trail,* p. 301.

69. Mildred Eversole, ed. "Richard Oglesby, Forty Niner," Illinois State Historical Society, Springfield (1938).

70. Curran, *Fearful Crossing,* p. 184.

71. Quoted in Thomas Hunt, "James Wilkins Diary," *Overland Journal* 8, no. 3 (1990): 32.

72. Langworthy, *Scenery of the Plains, Mountains and Mines,* p. 32.

73. Hunt, *Ghost Trails to California,* p. 146.

74. Stewart, *The California Trail,* p. 101.

75. Levy, "We Were Forty Niners Too," p. 32.

76. Schlissel, *Women's Diaries,* p. 189.